VEGAN • SOS-FREE

Bravo

EXPRESS!

NO SUGAR, OIL, OR SALT

Ramses Bravo

EXECUTIVE CHEF, TRUENORTH HEALTH CENTER

Book Publishing Company
Summertown, Tennessee

Library of Congress Cataloging-in-Publication Data

Names: Bravo, Ramses, author.
Title: Bravo express! / Ramses Bravo.
Description: Summertown, Tennessee : Book Publishing Company, [2019] |
   Includes index.
Identifiers: LCCN 2018060236 | ISBN 9781570673627 (pbk.)
Subjects: LCSH: Vegan cooking. | Salt-free diet—Recipes. | Sugar-free
   diet—Recipes. | Low-fat diet—Recipes. | LCGFT: Cookbooks.
Classification: LCC TX837 .B7558 2019 | DDC 641.5/6362—dc23
LC record available at https://lccn.loc.gov/2018060236

Front cover: Coconut Bites, *pg. 135;* Spicy Jicama Salad, *pg. 43;* Wild Rice and Spinach, *pg. 74;* Yellow Curry Lentils, *pg. 77*

Back cover: Pan-Roasted Zucchini and Carrot Balls, pg. 101; Baby Bok Choy and Macadamias, pg. 90; Spicy Soba Noodles, pg. 71; Steamed Asparagus and Artichoke Hearts, pg. 103; Peach-Blueberry Sorbet, pg. 145

We chose to print this title on responsibly harvested paper stock certified by the Forest Stewardship Council, an independent auditor of responsible forestry practices. For more information, visit us.fsc.org.

MIX
Paper from responsible sources
FSC® C001701

Food photography: Ramses Bravo
Cover photo: Alan Roettinger
Stock photography: 123 RF
Cover and interior design: John Wincek

Printed in Hong Kong

Book Publishing Company
PO Box 99
Summertown, TN 38483
888-260-8458
bookpubco.com

ISBN: 978-1-57067-362-7

24 23 22 21 20   2 3 4 5 6 7 8 9

Disclaimer: The information in this book is presented for educational purposes only. It isn't intended to be a substitute for the medical advice of a physician, dietitian, or other health-care professional.

Nutritional Analyses: The nutrient values provided for the recipes in this book are estimates only, calculated from the individual ingredients used in each recipe based on the nutritional data found for those ingredients. Optional items are not included. Nutrient content may vary based on methods of preparation, origin, and freshness of ingredients, product brands, and other factors.

CONTENTS

To my past, present, and perhaps future children.
And to Mother Earth as well!

Welcome to
BRAVO EXPRESS!

The concept behind this cookbook is very simple: healthy, delicious food made possible by using only a few ingredients and a few steps. That's it.

Who are these recipes ideal for? If you like simple-to-follow recipes, don't want to spend a lot of time in the kitchen, love delicious meals, want ideas for quickly transforming leftovers into great dishes, need a yummy dish to take to a party that no one would single out as "healthy," or just enjoy good food, then this is the cookbook for you. If you suffer from diabetes or high blood pressure, have a heart condition, are struggling with your weight, or simply want to improve your quality of life, then this is the book for you as well. May these recipes bring you joy and health! For more great food ideas, please visit Chef Bravo's website at bravopb.com

ACKNOWLEDGMENTS

A big thanks to Bob and Cynthia Holzapfel at Book Publishing Company for giving me the opportunity to make this book a reality and to Jo Stepaniak for being my editor a second time.

I want to express my gratitude to the many people at TrueNorth who have helped me in my journey. Thank you to my boss, Dr. Alan Goldhamer, for employing and putting up with me for as long as he has. To the amazing Dr. Csilla Veress, I'm so grateful for your contribution of the High-Immunity Broth for this book. You are a wonderful woman. To my staff, in particular my sous chef Mauricio, thank you so much for working so hard and taking care of all the little things that allowed me the time to sit down and write. To all the patients who inspired me to come up with this project, thank you so much. I hope this book is useful to you.

Last but not least, thank you to my family and close friends, who are always rooting for me.

My Story

I never grew up wanting to be a vegan chef. Hell, I didn't even know what "vegan" meant until I was in high school. At that age, I didn't understand why anyone wouldn't want to enjoy the flavor of perfectly crisp bacon or garlic-buttered shrimp. Growing up in my grandmother's kitchen and indulging in these and similar fine flavors is why I grew up wanting to be a chef—a *real* chef.

My mind was made up from an early age. In the fall of 1996, I headed to San Francisco to complete two years of cooking school. Right after that, I moved to the East Coast to do a chef's training program for four years. Essentially, if it moved, I learned how to cut it, cook it, and eat it. This process always involved plenty of salt, oil, butter, cream, and cheese. I had a great time, and I was doing what I loved. After completing my training, I returned to California and became the chef for a high-end hotel for four years. Pizza, veal, lobster, fancy cheeses, and certainly lots of wine flowed freely. I put on ten pounds per year, and at the end of my stay there, I was tipping the scale at over two hundred pounds. That's when the universe began to rattle me.

After the hotel was sold, I decided to move on and start my own catering business. During a class to get my certification in safe food handling, I got a phone call from one of my mother's friends who told me about a guy who was looking for a chef to run his vegan kitchen. Up to that point, dealing with any vegan customers meant serving them a plate of rice with steamed vegetables on top and hoping they'd never come back. But as I wanted to have a successful business, and I figured "vegan" might be something some of my clients might ask for, I thought, "I'm certainly not going vegan, but I could further my education." I took the bait, and I set up a time to meet my future boss.

He was so enthusiastic, so passionate and dedicated, and he truly believed that a vegan diet would be good for anyone. I thought, "What a nutcase! Why would anyone want to eat vegan the rest of their life?" To top it off, he told me that not only was the cuisine vegan, but I also couldn't use sugar. I was slightly shocked, but I've never been a big fan of candy.

To be courteous, I agreed to meet him once more. In our next meeting, we started talking numbers, staff, equipment, and whatnot. He also mentioned that I couldn't use oil, either. *What? No oil?* At this point I felt like I was in a Bugs Bunny cartoon. Out of sheer curiosity and amusement, I agreed to meet him one more time just to see how wacky this whole thing could be.

During our last meeting, we went over more details about the job and the potential growth of the business. It was then that he dropped the roof on me. "By the way," he said, "you can't use salt, either." What ran through my mind sounded something like this: "No salt? No salt? *No salt?* Did this guy seriously just say no salt? Doesn't he know that the first and most important aspect of cooking is to season food properly? Did he really just say no salt? This guy is definitely cuckoo. Maybe he's also about to tell me that I'll be cooking blindfolded or that I'll be cooking with one hand tied behind my back."

But my boss is a very smart guy. His thought process probably sounded something like this: "This guy seems like a capable enough chef. I want to hire him, but I don't want to scare him off too quickly. I won't drop the bomb on him all at once. I'll just feed it to him bit by bit. Otherwise, he's going to think that he has to cook blindfolded or with one hand tied behind his back."

Whatever his thought process was, he was a fish out of water. No way was I going to take a vegan job, and most certainly not a salt-free, oil-free, and sugar-free vegan job. Under normal circumstances, I would have told him, "Thanks for the offer. I'm going to think about it, and maybe I'll get back to you." But this crazy vegan guy had two things going for him, and he didn't even know about them. One, I'm a sucker for start-up projects. He was moving his business into a newer and bigger facility, and I would be opening the kitchen from the ground up. Two, I was scared that I might not generate enough income with my catering business to support my family, so a steady paycheck with a bump in pay compared to my previous job was certainly enticing.

But the man had just said, "No salt." How could I introduce myself as the chef to any customer and be able to stand up for my food when it had no flavor at all? I was so very close to turning down the job, but I accepted it with the idea of furthering my education, learning about vegan food, and getting out of there in six months. I knew if I stayed any longer than that, it would ruin my chefness.

I'm truly happy to report I've been the chef at TrueNorth Health Center for over a decade now. I'm very grateful for all that I have and will accomplish here.

You might think this is a heartwarming story and that as soon as I became a vegan chef I found my happily ever after. The truth is, that's the furthest thing from what really happened.

I took the job, and over the next two weeks, I cooked many dishes, but I would put a small portion of each dish aside and add a little bit of salt from a stash I kept hidden on a shelf. I would taste my dishes, and I figured that since all my new customers weren't used to the same level of salt that I was, we were tasting my food at about the same level of enjoyment. To my surprise, after two weeks, I no longer needed the salt to know whether or not my food was good. Within a few months, I had lost many of the extra pounds I was carrying, and I had a lot more energy to keep up with my daughter. I then began writing my first cookbook, *Bravo!*, and pulled the kitchen together bit by bit.

This may sound like the start of a great job, but the vegan novelty wore off quickly. A constant war raged daily in my head for the next five years. I would hear my inner critic put me down: "Why have you lowered your standards? Why are you wasting your talents? Why are you here, you fool?" I would try to argue that I had a steady income and that I was healthier. But it didn't take long for me to feel angry and ashamed for staying at a job where I didn't want to be. Every day I kept thinking, "Why am I here? This isn't what I trained for."

Facebook and other social media made me even more miserable because I saw my fellow chef friends working in great restaurants and making wonderful food. Adding insult to injury were the meal plans at TrueNorth, which meant from time to time I had to deliver plates of steamed vegetables or the occasional baked yam. Many people would greet me with great joy, and they would tell me how wonderful I was and that I was changing and even saving their lives. Even though that was a great compliment, all it did was enrage me more. "Why am I here? They can pull any random person off the street to bake a yam and do my job. What am I doing here?" This conversation went on and on inside my head for five years.

While all this was churning inside me, my life became a statistic: one of the 50 percent of marriages in America that end in divorce. I was at a very low point in my life. But I distinctly remember having one thought: "You're not special. You are suffering from the same problems that thousands of others are suffering from." So I surrendered to the idea (based on one of those cheer-you-up social media posts) that my life wasn't falling apart; it was falling into place. I decided to have one more conversation with the voice inside my head. "Either shut up or get another job, because we're not doing this anymore."

For the next two years, my life transformed into one filled with gratitude and joy. I discovered meditation, and I began to enrich my life with positive people and experiences. I hosted a radio show for a year called *The Love Kitchen*. I learned to be happy and to embrace who I was. I accepted the fact I would lose some of my chef skills as a by-product of being a happy vegan chef. It may not be what I had trained for, but I was not going to cling to my skills at the cost of my happiness.

Two years later, it all finally clicked together for me. I knew how to be a regular chef, and I had also become a damn good vegan chef. I didn't have to choose one or the other; I was both. I was twice the chef, not half of one. I can now engage in food conversations with any steak-and-potato-loving Joe and a raw-kale-salad fanatic at the same time. This is something no regular or vegan chef that I know can do. I am a happy man who has found his purpose in life. I can cook tasty "regular" food, and I can also cook delicious and healthy vegan food. I can give people everywhere ideas for how to eat healthier, no matter what kind of diet they follow, and thus I can help them improve their lives. So yes, this story has a happy ending, but don't get me wrong. Like I said, I'm not special at all. Without my daughter, this story could have easily crumbled. Without her, drugs and alcohol would have been easy to turn to, but I think kale and oatmeal (with the occasional naughty morsel) were better choices.

How *Bravo Express!* Came to Be

After about eight years being the chef at TrueNorth Health Center, I began to see a pattern in our guests. TrueNorth runs like a hotel. People check in, they get their room, and then we feed them delicious, healthy food. Every day they'll come to the dining room for breakfast, lunch, and dinner to enjoy a wide variety of flavor-packed meals.

Throughout the day we keep them busy with lectures, cooking demos, and movie nights, all focused on educating them about a healthy way of living. Our guests get daily housekeeping services and complimentary laundry service, and if they run out of things to do, they can book a massage, acupuncture, reflexology session, or even a facial treatment. Sounds nice and comfy, doesn't it?

But as I paid close attention to our guests, I began to notice something. They all got a bit anxious when it was time to go home. I could see it in their faces, and I could hear it in their tone of voice when they'd ask, "How do I do this when I get home?"

At first I would smile and tell them that everything would be okay. I told them they could stick to the diet if they really wanted to, and if they needed recipes, *Bravo!*, my first cookbook, was available if they hadn't purchased it yet. Week after week it would be the same, just different guests with a similar worry. Then suddenly it hit me. The people who come to TrueNorth are living outside of reality for a short amount of time. We prep everything for them, cook for them, and clean up after them, and they tend to do very well while they're in our care because we give them a lot of support. But once they're back home, they don't have breakfast ready and waiting for them when they wake up. They have to do their own laundry, and they also have to go back to work and back to dealing with kids and spouses who sometimes are not good support systems.

I thought I had at least taken care of the cooking part when I had written *Bravo!* But occasionally I received feedback from people who said that even though my recipes in the book are great, some of them have too many ingredients and some even require a two-day process. That's when the idea for *Bravo Express!* was born. I felt the need and obligation to provide a cookbook that isn't intimidating and can provide delicious, quick, and simple meals using only a few ingredients and calling for only a few steps. People going home after a stay at TrueNorth need a soft landing. And so here it is: *Bravo Express!*

The Philosophy behind the Diet

THE GENERAL PLAN

The diet I'm proposing for you is simple. It's a healthy diet that calls for minimal sacrifices. I call it the SOS-free whole-plant-foods diet. Now let me explain what this means:

- **SOS-free.** This refers to cooking without using refined salt (S), oil (O), or sugar (S), and not eating anything that contains them, including refined carbohydrates, such as breads, chips, cookies, crackers, and so forth.

- **Why no refined sugar?** Sweeteners and syrups, such as sugar, honey, maple syrup, and agave nectar, offer no nutritive value, stimulate the body's insulin response, and cause blood glucose levels to rise. Eating these sweeteners results in cravings and mood swings that can lead to overeating, obesity, and diseases of excess. The human body ages more quickly when it has to process too many empty calories. In addition, when have you seen a cake or a doughnut with sugar but without added fats, such as oil or butter?

- **Why no oil?** A diet high in refined oil increases the risk of diabetes. It also contributes a large number of empty calories. Plus, it forces you to eat more salt. When oil goes into your mouth, it acts as a blanket that prevents other flavors from being detected by your taste buds. Consequently, salt is needed to override this blanket and make food taste more flavorful. When you use oil in your food, it's almost impossible to avoid adding salt.

- **Why no salt?** Have you ever had a meal with people who grab the salt shaker and liberally sprinkle their food without tasting it first? Unfortunately, our bodies develop a tolerance to the taste of salt in food, but the addition of salt results in passive overeating and excess weight gain. Salt also elevates blood pressure, increasing the risk of heart attack, stroke, kidney disease, and osteoporosis.

- **Whole foods.** This refers to eating unrefined foods and whole grains, such as brown rice versus white rice, whole potatoes versus potato chips, whole greens versus shake powders, and whole dates versus maple syrup or agave nectar.

- **Plant foods.** This is simple—no animal products. It means no meat, no cheese, no milk, no cream, no eggs, no bacon (I know this is one of the hardest), and no seafood. If it had eyes (potatoes don't count), you leave it alone.

- **Do you have to be perfect at it?** No, I'm not asking you to be perfect. If I did, I would be setting you up for failure. Instead, I'm asking you to take an interest in your health and in the quality of your life. Yes, I know we're all going to eventually die of something. But during your golden years, do you want your pharmacist to know you by your first name because you have so many prescriptions that need to be filled on a regular basis? If there's an opportunity for sex, do you want to be able to rise (pun intended) to the occasion? Do you wish to keep your relationship with the toilet paper a private matter?

Make no mistake—all of the above factors can and will have a powerful effect on the quality of your life. The closer you adhere to being SOS-free, the trimmer, healthier, and happier you'll be.

Vegetable Broth and Sodium

The purpose of this book is to give you simple recipes that can be prepared quickly. If you make your own veggie broth at home, kudos to you. But if you decide it's more convenient to buy it at the store, make sure to get no-salt-added vegetable broth or a low-sodium version at the very least. Using regular commercial vegetable broth will significantly increase your sodium intake, and it will also change the intended flavor of the recipes.

ADVICE FROM THE CHEF
About Nutrition

Although a nutritional analysis for each recipe is provided, don't get too caught up in it. When it comes to food, it doesn't matter how nutritious it is if it doesn't taste good. You and I both know that. If it's not tasty, you're not going to eat it!

Mind Your Tongue

Recipes are nothing more than guidelines, so trust your instincts. If your taste buds tell you that a dish needs more lemon or garlic or pepper or something else (except for salt), then go ahead and add it to the dish. Remember, the most important thing about this diet is that you like it.

Loving Leftovers

There are some people who can eat leftovers every day of their lives (my dad, for example), while others can't even stand the word. Throwing away leftover food is a waste of money, but you can't force it down someone's throat. Instead, the trick is to give leftovers a makeover. Even just pouring a little sauce over left-over food can transform its appearance and taste. You'll find plenty of recipes in this book that provide opportunities to creatively use leftovers, such as Tacodillas (page 117), Noritos (page 113), and Buckwheat Tabbouleh (page 66).

Choosing the Right Onion

I'm often asked which onion is the right one to use. In general, there are two main considerations: color and comfort level.

All onions are similar in flavor, so you can substitute one for another without any major disasters. But the right color onion can definitely have an impact on the outcome. For example, for the Steamed Asparagus and Artichoke Hearts (page 103), I chose to use red onion because it provides an attractive color contrast with the bright-green asparagus. Visually, red onion makes this dish more appealing, even though in terms of flavor, it would be almost identical if yellow or white onion was used.

Now suppose you're making two recipes: one calls for shallots, and the other calls for leeks, but you only have yellow onions at home. It would require extra time and money to make a trip to the grocery store. Plus, pound for pound, shallots are more expensive than yellow onions, and leeks take more time to clean. Are you now more comfortable with going to the store or would you rather just use the yellow onions for both recipes? Don't worry; whichever choice you make will be the right one.

What's for Breakfast?

You might have noticed that there isn't a breakfast section in this book. You might also have noticed that on the sample two-week menu (page 20), fresh fruit is suggested for breakfast on most days, but greens and vegetables are also listed for a few days.

I encourage you to eat as many greens and veggies for breakfast as you desire. They are a pleasant change of pace, and they will make you feel proud and healthy when you start out your day eating them. But remember, this is the Bravo Express way of eating. If you like making smoothies in the morning because they're fast and easy, that's perfect!

If you like fruit but don't enjoy cutting it up in the morning, and there are only so many apples, pears, and bananas you can eat, then here's another suggestion. Grab a small seedless watermelon or a honeydew, cantaloupe, or papaya for breakfast. Rinse it first, of course, then cut it in half. Take a regular spoon out of your silverware drawer and use it to scoop out the seeds (skip this step for the watermelon). Then, with the same spoon, start scooping chunks of fruit into your mouth. No peeling necessary. Once you're done eating all the fruit, simply discard the single piece of empty peel into the trash or compost bin. Now *that's* a Bravo Express type of breakfast.

Getting Started in the Bravo Express Kitchen

ESSENTIAL EQUIPMENT

Here is a list of all the equipment you'll need to make the recipes in this book. If you have a well-stocked kitchen, you probably have most of these items already on hand.

- 1 wooden cutting board, about 20 x 16 inches *(for fruits and vegetables, except onions, garlic, and ginger)*
- 1 small cutting board, about 10 x 5 inches *(use this exclusively for onions, garlic, and ginger so your fruits don't pick up unwanted flavors)*
- 1 sharp 8-inch chef's knife with a fitted knife guard *(see "Taking Care of Your Knives," page 12)*
- 1 serrated paring knife with a fitted knife guard
- 2 pots with lids, 4 quart and 2 quart
- 2 sauté pans, 10 inch and 8 inch
- 2 baking sheets, 18 x 13 inches and 13 x 9 inches
- 2 silicone baking mats *(such as Silpat brand)* to fit your baking sheets
- 1 steamer basket *(preferably the retractable kind)*

- 1 wooden spoon
- 1 solid metal spoon
- 1 slotted metal spoon
- 1 silicone spatula
- 1 metal spatula
- 1 ladle
- 1 whisk
- 1 Microplane zester
- 1 citrus juicer
- 1 can opener
- 1 peeler
- 1 melon baller
- 1 set of measuring cups
- 1 set of measuring spoons
- 1 Japanese mandoline
- 1 food processor
- 1 high-speed blender

TAKING CARE OF YOUR KNIVES

A knife should always be stored clean, with its knife guard in place. After you're done using a knife, immediately wash and dry it, put the knife guard back on, and put the knife away. Never put a knife in the sink, the dishwasher, or a drawer full of other tools where it can get banged around, bent, or chipped by other metal objects. **Never!**

Although knife blocks may seem like a good place to store knives, they are extremely unsanitary. Instead, use a knife guard for each one of your knives; they're very inexpensive (and replacing high-quality knives is costly).

Bravo Express
Cooking Fundamentals

THE ART OF DRY SAUTÉING

By definition, *sauté* means to fry quickly in a little hot fat. Such is the practice of putting oil or butter in a pan before adding food, and it's widely accepted that this is the only way to sauté. But just because everyone else seems to be doing it this way doesn't mean you have to!

Allow me to introduce a new concept: dry sautéing. This means to sauté without using any oil. *Say what?* I get it. This new concept may sound strange to you. You might fear that sautéing without oil can't be done because the food will burn and stick to the pan. But let me assure you that I have been dry sautéing both on the job and at home since 2007, and it works every time. I invite you to be one of the few who know how to sauté in a much healthier way.

How to do it: Preheat the pot or sauté pan for a couple of minutes. You'll know that it's ready to go when you put your hand near the inside bottom of the pot or pan (without touching it!) and can feel that it's hot. Put the veggies in the pan as instructed in the recipe. You should instantly hear a sizzle that's almost identical to the sound of sautéing with oil.

Why it works: When each piece of onion, celery, mushroom, or other veggie starts to heat up inside a hot pan, it begins to release its water content. You'll notice that as the veggies cook, steam escapes from the pan. This small bit of water coming out of the veggies prevents them from burning or sticking. Eventually, enough water will evaporate that the veggies, along with the bottom of the pan, will begin to brown nicely. This process will always give you a wide enough window to dry sauté your veggies without burning them.

THE ART OF WET SAUTÉING

Just as veggies can be browned by dry sautéing, they can also be cooked by wet sautéing. It's the yin to the yang.

How to do it: Start by putting 2 to 3 tablespoons of no-salt-added vegetable broth or water in a cold pot or sauté pan. Add the ingredients as directed in the recipe and proceed to cook, never allowing any browning to occur. If the ingredients begin to dry out and the possibility of browning occurs before the food has finished cooking, simply add a bit more broth or water and continue.

Why you'd want to do it: Wet sautéing should be used when you don't want any browning to occur. For example, the recipe for Yellow Bell Pepper Soup (page 32) calls for wet sautéing. The goal for that particular recipe is to keep as much of the vibrant yellow color of the bell pepper as possible. If dry sautéing were used and the veggies browned, the color of the soup would be less attractive. Imagine making a cauliflower puree or a potato-leek soup. You'd want to keep those as white as possible; therefore, you would choose wet over dry sautéing.

GETTING YOUR BEANS ON

I'll be honest—canned beans are not my favorites. I'd rather cook beans from scratch, but I know that contradicts the whole idea of simple and easy recipes. So, as long as I can get enough flavor into canned beans, they can actually work. However, if you are dead set against canned beans for whatever reason, here's my procedure for cooking dried beans from scratch.

1. Spread the dried beans on a rimmed baking sheet and remove any stones or other debris.

2. Transfer the beans to a large strainer or colander and thoroughly rinse them under cold running water.

3. Put the beans in a large bowl or pot and add enough cold water to cover the beans by at least six inches.

4. Let the beans soak at room temperature for 8 to 12 hours. (It's easiest to do this overnight.)

5. Drain the beans in a colander.

6. Put the beans in a large pot with no-salt-added vegetable broth using a 4:1 ratio (4 parts broth to 1 part beans).

7. Cook over medium-high heat, keeping the liquid at a simmer (don't allow it to boil) until the beans are soft, about 1½ hours. Keep a close eye on the beans, and use a ladle during the first 45 minutes to discard any foam that accumulates on the top. The liquid that remains after the beans are cooked can be used as vegetable broth.

PRECISION BAKING

People always want to know exactly how long to cook things in the oven. Basically, food should cook in the oven until it looks good enough to eat, and not a second before or after that.

Picture this. Suppose you write a recipe for me, and your recipe states to put the vegetables on a baking sheet and bake in the oven at 350 degrees for 15 minutes. You might think that is precise information, but in reality, these instructions are vague. The reason is that every oven is different. They all have hot spots, and many of them are not properly calibrated. My oven at work is a big, shiny, expensive commercial appliance that's supposed to cook food evenly. It also has four shiny metal racks. But the top rack has a hot spot in the back, the second rack has a hot spot in the front, the entire third rack is the cold spot in the oven, and the bottom rack has a hot spot in the front. Clearly you can see what the problem is. Your recipe could only give me so much information, and you couldn't give me any more precise information because when you wrote the recipe, you had no idea that my oven is so wacky.

So I apologize to you because I couldn't possibly give you precise information for how long to cook things in your oven since every oven is different. The oven times in my recipes are simply suggestions—starting points. Trust your eyes and your sense of smell. When the food looks good enough for you to eat it, that's when it's ready. It could be five minutes more or five minutes less than I suggest because your oven might run hotter or colder than mine. Also, if you have multiple items baking at the same time, the cooking time will increase, and every time you open the oven door, the temperature drops, so that too will prolong the cooking time.

HOW TO . . .

Roast Garlic

Preheat the oven to 350 degrees F. Arrange peeled garlic cloves on a rimmed baking sheet in a single layer. Roast until golden brown, 12–15 minutes.

Stored in a sealed container in the refrigerator, roasted garlic will keep for 2 weeks.

Toast Nuts and Seeds

Preheat the oven to 350 degrees F. Spread the nuts or seeds on a rimmed baking sheet in a single layer. Toast until golden brown, 3–5 minutes.

To Toast or Not to Toast

I'm often asked whether raw or toasted nuts and seeds are better. For me the answer is simple. Toasted nuts and seeds will always have more flavor. For that reason I prefer them over raw, even if it takes a bit more time in the kitchen. The extra flavor is definitely worth it.

Toast Spices

Your cooking will benefit greatly if you toast spices before using them. Toasting opens up the spices and releases their flavor and aroma. To toast spices, simply put them (whole or ground, depending on what the recipe calls for) in a sauté pan over medium-high heat, stirring frequently, for 1–2 minutes. Immediately remove them from the heat so they don't overcook. They are then ready to be used.

Toast Coconut

To toast unsweetened shredded dried coconut, preheat the oven to 400 degrees F. Spread the coconut in a single layer on a baking sheet and bake for 2 minutes. Remove from the oven, stir, spread back into a single layer, and return to the oven until evenly toasted, 1–2 minutes longer. The whole process should take 3–4 minutes, but trust your eyes more than the time.

Cut Corn Kernels from the Cob

Shuck the corn. Stand one cob at a time in the center of a two-quart container. Holding the upper tip of the cob, use a sharp paring knife to slice downward from the top of the cob. The kernels will fall into the container. Rotate the cob and repeat until all the kernels have been cut off.

Clean and Use Leeks

It's very important to remove all the dirt from leeks, which seem to collect much more dirt than you can see. Trim off the root ends and tough green parts of the leaves. Use only the tender white and light-green parts of the leeks in recipes. Cut the leeks as needed for the recipe and put them in a strainer. Rinse thoroughly under running water for 30–40 seconds, making sure that all surfaces of the leeks are rinsed well and no dirt or grit remains between the layers.

THE BUILDING BLOCKS OF THE BRAVO EXPRESS DIET

In order to stay alive, humans know they better get enough to eat. That's why we created drive-through restaurants, which not only make it easy to obtain food but also make it easy to consume more than our bodies require. As you no doubt know, eating fast food is notoriously unhealthy. The alternative is to cook all your meals from scratch at home, but that typically means spending a whole lot of time in the kitchen. Needless to say, that's not always a great option. So what's the key to making food healthy, easy, and quick? Starchy vegetables and whole grains!

These foods will fill your belly and keep you satisfied while ensuring that your calorie requirements are met but not exceeded. They make perfect sense for the Bravo Express kitchen because they are so simple to cook. And best of all, they can help you balance your budget as well as your weight. It's true that eating a whole-plant diet can become expensive, especially if you buy organic. But if a significant portion of your diet is based on starchy vegetables and whole grains, your wallet will breathe a sigh of relief.

The following is a list of all these wonderful food items, along with instructions for how to cook them. Yes, most of them take a while to cook, but they don't require constant attention. All you need to do is listen for the timer go off while you're busy doing something else. Ideally, you should always cook extra. That way, you'll only have to heat up the oven once, but you'll have enough food for multiple meals.

Baked Potatoes

You can bake any kind of potato, such as Yukon gold, red skinned, purple, or russet. Preheat the oven to 350 degrees F. Put the whole potatoes directly on the oven rack (or on a rimmed baking sheet if they're very small) and bake for

40–50 minutes, depending on their size. Alternatively, cut the potatoes in half, sprinkle the cut side with seasoning if you like, and bake skin-side down for 25–30 minutes, depending on their size. Baked potatoes are done when a paring knife slides in and out with no resistance.

Steamed Potatoes

To steam whole potatoes, put them in a pot with water and a steamer insert. Cover and cook over medium heat for 25–35 minutes, depending on their size. If you cut the potatoes in half, you can decrease the cooking time to 15–20 minutes, again depending on their size. Steamed potatoes are done when a paring knife slides in and out with no resistance. Peeling won't affect the cooking time of potatoes, but I advise against peeling purple potatoes when steaming them, as the peel helps to retain their vibrant color.

Baked Yams and Sweet Potatoes

Preheat the oven to 350 degrees F. Line a baking sheet with parchment paper or a silicone baking mat and arrange the whole yams or sweet potatoes on it. The lined baking sheet will catch any syrup that's released from the yams or sweet potatoes during baking and prevent it from burning onto the sheet. It will also make cleanup a whole lot easier. Snip the ends off the yams or sweet potatoes, as this will allow more water to evaporate while they bake, which will make them more dense and meaty. Bake for 40–50 minutes, depending on their size. Alternatively, cut the yams or sweet potatoes in half, sprinkle the cut side with seasoning if you like, and bake skin-side down for 25–30 minutes. Baked yams or sweet potatoes are done when a paring knife slides in and out with no resistance.

Steamed Yams and Sweet Potatoes

I don't tend to steam yams or sweet potatoes whole because by the time the center is fully cooked, the outer part is too mushy. Although the flavor isn't affected, it has an off texture for me, but *chacun à son goût* (to each his own). Put the whole yams or sweet potatoes in a pot with water and a steamer insert. Cover and cook over medium heat for 25–35 minutes, depending on their size. If you cut the yams or sweet potatoes in half, you can decrease the cooking time to 15–20 minutes, again depending on their size. Steamed yams and sweet potatoes are done when a paring knife slides in and out with no resistance.

Microwaved Potatoes, Yams, and Sweet Potatoes

Yes, potatoes, yams, and sweet potatoes can be cooked in a microwave, and microwaving them actually fits with the Bravo Express philosophy. However, when cooked this way, their texture may be a bit strange. Also, many people think it's unhealthy to cook anything in a microwave. If you want to use your microwave anyway, then cook the potatoes according to the manufacturer's instructions. They are done when a paring knife slides in and out with no resistance. If you're wondering whether I do or don't use a microwave, I will tell you that I never, ever, cook anything in the microwave, but I do use it to reheat food.

Brown, Red, and Forbidden Black Rice

Put the rice in a pot with no-salt-added vegetable broth, using a 2:1 ratio (2 parts broth to 1 part rice) and bring to a boil over high heat. Stir the rice once, cover the pot, and turn the heat down to low. Cook for 35 minutes. One cup of dry rice will yield about 3 cups cooked.

Quinoa

Put the quinoa in a pot with no-salt-added vegetable broth using a 2:1 ratio (2 parts broth to 1 part quinoa) and bring to a boil over high heat. Stir the quinoa once, cover the pot, and turn the heat down to low. Cook for 25 minutes. One cup of dry quinoa will yield about 3 cups cooked.

Buckwheat

Put the buckwheat in a pot with no-salt-added vegetable broth using a 2:1 ratio (2 parts broth to 1 part buckwheat) and bring to a boil over high heat. Stir the buckwheat once, cover the pot, and turn the heat down to low. Cook for 15 minutes. One cup of dry buckwheat will yield about 2½ cups cooked.

Wild Rice

Wild rice is technically not a rice but a grass. If you've ever cooked pasta, you already know how to cook wild rice. Put the wild rice in a pot with no-salt-added vegetable broth using a 4:1 ratio (4 parts broth to 1 part wild rice) and bring to a boil over high heat. Immediately turn down the heat so the broth stays at a simmer. Cook, stirring occasionally, until tender, about 40 minutes. When the wild rice is fully cooked, drain the rice in a strainer to remove the excess liquid. One cup of dry wild rice will yield about 3 cups cooked.

PREP DAY

Prep day is when you set yourself up for success by preparing in advance the food you'll need for the week. Designating a day of the week to roast garlic, peel onions, bake yams, freeze fruit for ice cream, and cook grains and dried beans will help cut down on the time you need to spend in the kitchen when your schedule is tight or you just don't feel like cooking. Although prep day isn't essential, you'll be glad to have most of your ingredients ready to go so that all you have to do is open the fridge and grab what you need.

SAMPLE MENUS FOR TWO WEEKS

The following sample menus don't include every recipe from this book. They are simply meant to give you some ideas for getting started and show you how to minimize your time in the kitchen. An asterisk (*) next to an item indicates that you should double the recipe, as you'll need to use it again a day or two later. Day 1 for each week is designated as a prep day. Although the list of items that need to be prepped may seem long, you will mainly just need to put the food in the oven and wait for it to cook.

Week 1

WEEK 1	DAY 1 PREP

- Preheat the oven to 350 degrees F and roast tomatoes, onions, and garlic cloves (*see page 15*) for Smoky Tomato Dressing (*page 59*) and Bravo Express Salsa (*page 129*).
- Roast extra garlic cloves for Pecan Gremolata (*page 125*) and Roasted-Garlic Mashed Potatoes (*page 69*).
- Toast cashews, macadamia nuts, pecans, and sesame seeds (*see page 16*) for Lettuce Wraps (*page 112*), Baby Bok Choy and Macadamias (*page 90*), Pecan Gremolata (*page 125*), and Mango-Ginger Dressing (*page 51*), respectively.
- Toast coconut (*see page 16*) for Coconut Bites (*page 135*).
- Freeze fruit for Peach-Blueberry Sorbet (*page 145*).

- Cook dried fruit for Date-Apricot Paste (*page 142*).
- Peel and dice butternut squash for Butternut Squash and Kale Soup (*page 28*).

WEEK 1	DAY 1 MENU

Breakfast Cider-Steamed Swiss Chard (*page 91*)

Lunch Cream of Corn Soup* (*page 31*) and green salad with Smoky Tomato Dressing (*page 59*)

Snack Melon Skewers with Orange Syrup (*page 147*)

Dinner Caraway-Mustard Kidney Beans (*page 83*) and Roasted-Garlic Mashed Potatoes* (*page 69*)

WEEK 1	DAY 2 MENU

Breakfast Fresh fruit

Lunch Spicy Soba Noodles (*page 71*) and baked yams (*see page 18*)

Snack Spiced Pine Nuts (*page 119*)

Dinner Butternut Squash and Kale Soup (*page 28*) and buckwheat* (*see page 19*) with Bravo Express Pesto (*page 121*)

WEEK 1	DAY 3 MENU

Breakfast Oven-Roasted Plantain Fajitas (*page 65*)

Lunch Cream of Corn Soup (*page 31*) and Baby Bok Choy and Macadamias (*page 90*)

Snack Peach-Blueberry Sorbet (*page 145*)

Dinner Brussels Sprouts and Dried Figs (*page 92*) and Tacodillas (*page 117*) with Chipotle-Almond Salsa (*page 126*)

WEEK 1	DAY 4 MENU

Breakfast Fresh fruit

Lunch Buckwheat Tabbouleh (*page 66*) and Lettuce Wraps (*page 112*)

Snack Date-Apricot Paste (*page 142*) with celery sticks

Dinner Orange-Braised Fennel (*page 88*), Pan-Roasted Zucchini and Carrot Balls (*page 101*), and brown rice* (*see page 19*)

Breakfast Lemon-Garlic Broccolini *(page 94)*

Lunch Potato-Broccoli Soup *(page 35)* and Noritos *(page 113)*

Snack Creamy Tofu *(page 86)* and rice crackers

Dinner Sweet Winter Squash Slaw *(page 47)*, Cajun-Roasted Navy Beans and Mushrooms *(page 78)*, and Coconut Bites *(page 135)*

| **WEEK 1** | **DAY 6 MENU** |

Breakfast Fresh fruit

Lunch Coriander-Spiced Roots and Pintos *(page 81)* and green salad with Lemon-Parsley Dressing* *(page 57)*

Snack Garbanzo Crunch* *(page 80)*

Dinner Carrot-Ginger Soup* *(page 29)*, Tempeh Tacos *(page 114)*, and Rajas *(page 99)*

| **WEEK 1** | **DAY 7 MENU** |

Breakfast Banana and Flaxseed Polenta *(page 73)*

Lunch Oven-Roasted Red Kuri Squash *(page 102)* and Pecan Gremolata *(page 125)*

Snack Spicy Apple Cider *(page 137)*

Dinner Roasted Cactus Fingers *(page 97)*, Indian-Spiced Baked Beans *(page 85)*, and green salad with Strawberry Balsamic Dressing *(page 53)*

Week 2

- Preheat the oven to 350 degrees F and roast garlic cloves (*see page 15*) for Roasted-Garlic Mashed Potatoes (*page 69*) and Cashew Cream (*page 122*).
- Toast sesame seeds, coconut, walnuts, and cashews (*see page 16*) for Hearty Balsamic Hummus (*page 84*), Yam Empanadas (*page 118*), Wild Rice and Spinach (*page 74*), and Blueberry-Lime Truffles (*page 138*), respectively.
- Freeze bananas for Banana-Walnut Ice Cream (*page 146*) and mangoes for Mango-Coconut Ice Cream (*page 143*).

Breakfast Fresh fruit

Lunch Grilled Hearts of Palm Salad (*page 45*)

Snack Pickled Watermelon (*page 41*)

Dinner Roasted Parsnips and Shallots* (*page 96*), Cider-Steamed Swiss Chard (*page 91*), and quinoa (*see page 19*)

Breakfast Fresh Fruit

Lunch Cream of Spinach Soup (*page 27*) and baked potatoes (*see page 17*)

Snack Banana-Walnut Ice Cream (*page 146*)

Dinner Ginger-Steamed Eggplant (*page 98*), baked yams* (*see page 18*), and green salad with Datey Mustard Dressing (*page 54*)

Breakfast Cider-Steamed Swiss Chard (*page 91*)

Lunch Steamed potatoes (*see page 18*) and Avocado and Grapefruit Salad (*page 40*)

Snack Mango-Coconut Ice Cream (*page 143*)

Dinner Yellow Bell Pepper Soup (*page 32*), Savory Lentil Crêpes (*page 108*), and Hearty Balsamic Hummus (*page 84*)

WEEK 2	DAY 4 MENU

Breakfast Fresh Fruit

Lunch Grilled Plums with Baby Arugula *(page 38)*

Snack Baked yams *(see page 18)* with Honeydew Crème Anglaise *(page 132)*

Dinner Radicchio and Persimmon Salad *(page 44)*, Yellow Curry Lentils *(page 77)*, and wild rice* *(see page 19)*

WEEK 2	DAY 5 MENU

Breakfast Sweet Lentil Crêpes *(page 111)* with Berry Marmalade* *(page 124)*

Lunch Wild Rice and Spinach *(page 74)* and Steamed Asparagus and Artichoke Hearts *(page 103)*

Snack Blueberry-Lime Truffles *(page 138)*

Dinner Cilantro-Buttered Corn *(page 63)* and Quick Steamed Kale and Mushrooms *(page 106)*

WEEK 2	DAY 6 MENU

Breakfast Fresh Fruit

Lunch Roasted-Garlic Mashed Potatoes *(page 69)* and Roasted Cauliflower and Peas *(page 104)*

Snack Yam Fries *(page 68)*

Dinner Curried Apples and Watercress Salad *(page 46)*, baked potatoes *(see page 17)* with Cashew Cream *(page 122)*, and Yam Empanadas *(page 118)*

WEEK 2	DAY 7 MENU

Breakfast Baked Spiced Apples *(page 141)* with Raw Cranberry-Orange Relish *(page 128)*

Lunch Edamame and Kale Salad *(page 48)* and steamed sweet potatoes *(see page 18)*

Snack Spicy Jicama Salad *(page 43)*

Dinner Braised Red Cabbage with Dried Cherries *(page 93)* and baked potatoes *(see page 17)* with Tomatillo Dressing *(page 58)*

SOUPS

Making great soup is an art. Often homemade soups call for many ingredients and long cooking times, but I made it a point to include some soup recipes that come together fast, because everyone loves soup, especially on a cold, rainy day. If you find a good no-salt-added vegetable broth (or if you make your own) and you use high-quality produce, even a quick soup can be delicious. Keep in mind that soup is always tastier the day after it's made; letting it rest gives the flavors a chance to marry. And since leftover soup is always better, make extra whenever you can.

Cream of Spinach Soup

cream of
SPINACH SOUP

 his soup is a terrific way to get your daily dose of greens without having to eat them raw. For a different twist, replace the spinach with an equal amount of kale.

½ cup chopped shallots

2 tablespoons chopped garlic

6 cups no-salt-added vegetable broth

½ cup raw cashews

4 cups spinach, firmly packed

1 Dry sauté the shallots and garlic in a medium pot over medium heat for 3 minutes.

2 Add the broth and cashews and bring to a simmer. Cook for 5 minutes.

3 Transfer to a blender. Add the spinach and process until smooth. Serve hot.

	CALORIES	PROTEIN	FAT	CARBOHYDRATE	DIETARY FIBER	CALCIUM	SODIUM
per serving	310	12g	15g	31g	5g	220mg	141mg

butternut squash
AND KALE SOUP

 *A**dding the ginger at the end of the cooking time preserves its spicy kick, which beautifully complements the sweetness of the squash.*

4 cups diced butternut squash

2 cups chopped kale, firmly packed

2 cups diced yellow onions

8 cups no-salt-added vegetable broth

2 tablespoons peeled and chopped fresh ginger

1 Dry sauté the squash, kale, and onions in a medium pot over medium heat for 5 minutes.

2 Add the broth and bring to a simmer. Cook for 15 minutes.

3 Transfer to a blender. Add the ginger and process until smooth. Serve hot.

	CALORIES	PROTEIN	FAT	CARBOHYDRATE	DIETARY FIBER	CALCIUM	SODIUM
per serving	143	3g	0g	32g	5g	131mg	23mg

carrot-ginger **SOUP**

 uckily, *carrots are available year-round. That means you can serve this soup cold on a really hot summer's day or piping hot during a cold winter's night.*

4 cups sliced carrots

2 cups chopped leeks (white and light-green parts only)

½ cup carrot juice

8 cups no-salt-added vegetable broth

¼ cup peeled and chopped fresh ginger

1 kaffir lime leaf, or zest of 1 lime

1   Dry sauté the carrots and leeks in a large pot, stirring frequently, until the vegetables and the bottom of the pot are browned.

2   Deglaze the pot with the carrot juice and cook, stirring frequently, until the juice evaporates.

3   Add the broth and bring to a simmer. Cook for 15 minutes.

4   Transfer to a blender. Add the ginger and kaffir lime leaf and process until smooth. Serve hot.

	CALORIES	PROTEIN	FAT	CARBOHYDRATE	DIETARY FIBER	CALCIUM	SODIUM
per serving	141	3g	1g	30g	5g	78mg	106mg

mushroom **SOUP**

 A ny single type of mushroom can be used for this recipe, but for the best flavor possible, use a mixture of different varieties, such as chanterelle, oyster, portobello, and shiitake.

4 cups sliced mushrooms

1 large red onion, sliced

2 tablespoons chopped garlic

2 tablespoons red wine vinegar

6 cups no-salt-added vegetable broth

Chopped fresh thyme (optional)

1 Dry sauté the mushrooms, onion, and garlic in a medium pot over medium-high heat until the vegetables and the bottom of the pot are browned.

2 Add the vinegar and stir until it evaporates.

3 Add the broth and bring to a simmer. Cook for 15 minutes.

4 Garnish with the optional thyme just before serving. Serve hot.

	CALORIES	PROTEIN	FAT	CARBOHYDRATE	DIETARY FIBER	CALCIUM	SODIUM
per serving	61	3g	0g	11g	2g	17mg	7mg

CREAM OF corn soup

 resh corn is sweetest in late summer and early fall. But this recipe can be made year-round by substituting frozen or canned corn when fresh isn't available.

4 ears fresh corn, kernels removed (see page 16), 4 cups thawed frozen corn, or 4 cups drained canned corn

2 leeks (white and light-green parts only), thinly sliced

3 shallots, thinly sliced

4 garlic cloves, minced

6 cups no-salt-added vegetable broth

1 tablespoon thinly sliced fresh sage (optional)

1 Wet sauté the corn, leeks, shallots, and garlic in a medium pot over medium heat, stirring occasionally, for 5 minutes, making sure the vegetables don't brown.

2 Add the broth and bring to a simmer. Cook for 10 minutes.

3 Transfer to a blender and process until smooth.

4 Garnish with the optional sage just before serving. Serve hot.

	CALORIES	PROTEIN	FAT	CARBOHYDRATE	DIETARY FIBER	CALCIUM	SODIUM
per serving	195	6g	2g	42g	5g	44mg	34mg

yellow bell
PEPPER SOUP

*M*ake friends with the produce staff at your store and tell them you want to avoid hot-house peppers because they don't have as much flavor as those grown outdoors. Yellow tomatoes are a good alternative for yellow peppers in this recipe.

4 cups diced yellow bell peppers

1 cup diced fennel

½ cup diced shallots

3 cups no-salt-added vegetable broth

1 cup asparagus tips

1 Wet sauté the bell peppers, fennel, and shallots in a medium pot over medium heat for 3 minutes.

2 Add the broth and bring to a simmer. Cook for 5 minutes.

3 Transfer to a blender and process until smooth.

4 Garnish with the asparagus tips just before serving. Serve hot.

CHEF'S TIP: If your fennel has the tops (the little sprigs that look like dill), you can use them as a garnish for this soup in place of or in addition to the asparagus tips.

	CALORIES	PROTEIN	FAT	CARBOHYDRATE	DIETARY FIBER	CALCIUM	SODIUM
per serving	89	3g	1g	20g	3g	47mg	18mg

Yellow Bell Pepper Soup

heirloom
TOMATO SOUP

 Regular tomatoes can be used for this recipe, but the high sugar content and low acidity of heirloom tomatoes makes them ideal to use in this soup.

1 large red onion, julienned

8 garlic cloves, roasted (see page 15)

3 pounds ripe heirloom tomatoes, coarsely chopped

2 cups no-salt-added vegetable broth

Freshly ground black pepper

½ cup halved cherry tomatoes

Fresh basil leaves

1. Dry sauté the onion in a medium pot over medium heat until it begins to brown.
2. Add the garlic, heirloom tomatoes, and broth and bring to a simmer. Cook, stirring occasionally, for 8–10 minutes.
3. Transfer to a blender and process on high speed for 1 minute. Strain.
4. Season with pepper to taste.
5. Garnish with the cherry tomatoes and basil leaves.

	CALORIES	PROTEIN	FAT	CARBOHYDRATE	DIETARY FIBER	CALCIUM	SODIUM
per serving	98	4g	1g	21g	5g	63mg	21mg

potato-broccoli **SOUP**

 egular broccoli works well in this soup, but for an added punch of flavor, use broccolini, also known as baby broccoli, instead.

2 cups diced potatoes

2 cups broccoli florets

2 cups chopped leeks (white and light-green parts only)

2 tablespoons chopped garlic

½ teaspoon fennel seeds, toasted (see page 16)

½ teaspoon crushed red chile flakes

6 cups no-salt-added vegetable broth

1   Dry sauté the potatoes, broccoli, leeks, garlic, fennel seeds, and chile flakes in a medium pot over medium heat for 5 minutes.

2   Add the broth and bring to a simmer. Cook for 10 minutes.

3   Transfer to a blender and pulse for a few seconds to keep a chunky texture. Serve hot.

	CALORIES	PROTEIN	FAT	CARBOHYDRATE	DIETARY FIBER	CALCIUM	SODIUM
per serving	99	3g	0g	20g	3g	63mg	30mg

HIGH-IMMUNITY broth

*I*f you're not feeling well, drink this broth four times a day. It will boost your immune system in just a few days. Its healing properties include antibacterial, antimicrobial, antioxidant, anti-inflammatory, antiviral, disinfectant, immune boosting, and immune modulating. It's also surprisingly tasty and simple to make.

3 quarts water

1 cup chopped onion

1 cup mushroom stems or diced mushrooms

½ cup garlic cloves

½ cup chopped fresh ginger (unpeeled)

6 rosemary sprigs

6 thyme sprigs

1 Put all the ingredients in a large pot over high heat and bring to a boil.

2 Decrease the heat to medium-low and simmer gently for 15 minutes.

3 Strain before serving.

	CALORIES	PROTEIN	FAT	CARBOHYDRATE	DIETARY FIBER	CALCIUM	SODIUM
per serving	84	2g	0g	17g	3g	108mg	28mg

SALADS

2

I don't know why some people have a negative attitude toward salads. Maybe it's because the idea of a mouthful of lettuce, tomato, and cucumber seems so boring. Instead of that tired old song, think of a salad as a combination of flavors, colors, and textures. A salad should be as appealing to the eye as to the tongue, so your guests will be willing to try it. It should also include multiple flavor profiles, so it will intrigue the taste buds. And finally, a salad should contain a variety of textures that will delight the palate and inspire everyone to eat a full portion.

grilled plums
WITH BABY ARUGULA

 ther stone fruits, such as peaches or nectarines, can be used in this recipe if you don't have access to plums or if you simply prefer them.

4 ripe plums, cut in half and pitted

2 small red onions, sliced

2 tablespoons sherry vinegar

2 tablespoons no-salt-added vegetable broth

4 cups baby arugula, lightly packed

Freshly ground black pepper

1 Put the plums flesh-side down and the onions in a single layer on a hot grill for 3–4 minutes per side.

2 Put half the grilled onions in a food processor. Add the vinegar and broth and process for 20 seconds. Pour into a medium bowl.

3 Add the grilled plums, remaining grilled onions, and arugula and toss gently.

4 Season with pepper to taste. Serve immediately.

	CALORIES	PROTEIN	FAT	CARBOHYDRATE	DIETARY FIBER	CALCIUM	SODIUM
per serving	53	1g	0g	13g	2g	40mg	13mg

kelp NOODLE SALAD

 Although they look like thin strands of clear plastic, kelp noodles have a pleasant crunchy texture and salty flavor, so don't let their appearance fool you.

1½ cups quartered mushrooms (such as white button or cremini)

¼ cup thinly sliced red onion

¼ cup rice vinegar

2 cups kelp noodles

2 cups pea shoots or sunflower sprouts, lightly packed

1 teaspoon sesame seeds, toasted (see page 16)

1 Dry sauté the mushrooms in a large sauté pan over high heat for 3–4 minutes. Remove from the heat and let cool.

2 Put the onion and vinegar in a medium bowl and let marinate for 3–4 minutes.

3 Add the mushrooms, kelp noodles, pea shoots, and sesame seeds and stir until well combined. Serve immediately.

	CALORIES	PROTEIN	FAT	CARBOHYDRATE	DIETARY FIBER	CALCIUM	SODIUM
per serving	124	6g	1g	23g	5g	630mg	154mg

avocado and
GRAPEFRUIT SALAD

T o know if an avocado is ripe, try to remove the stem nub. If it doesn't come off easily, the avocado isn't ready, so pick a different one. If it does comes off easily, look at the hole left behind. If it looks bright green, the avocado is ripe and ready to eat. If you see any brown in the hole, the avocado will be brown inside as well.

4 ripe avocados, cut into quarters

2 grapefruits, segmented

2 cups sliced celery

2 cups baby arugula, lightly packed

1 cup pomegranate seeds or raspberries

½ cup whole fresh mint leaves, lightly packed

1   Divide the avocado equally among four plates.

2   Put the grapefruit segments, celery, arugula, pomegranate seeds, and mint leaves in a large bowl and stir until well combined.

3   Spoon the grapefruit mixture equally over the avocado. Serve immediately.

	CALORIES	PROTEIN	FAT	CARBOHYDRATE	DIETARY FIBER	CALCIUM	SODIUM
per serving	352	5g	22.5g	40g	16g	93mg	55mg

PICKLED watermelon

 ripe watermelon should feel heavy for its size. Ideally, it will have a yellow spot where it sat on the ground, and it shouldn't have any soft spots.

1 medium watermelon (8–10 pounds), cut into 2-inch cubes

½ cup diced red onion

½ cup chopped fresh cilantro, lightly packed

¼ cup unsweetened pineapple juice

¼ cup rice vinegar

Freshly ground black pepper

1 Put the watermelon, onion, cilantro, pineapple juice, and vinegar in a large bowl.

2 Stir until well combined, taking care to not smash the watermelon pieces.

3 Let marinate for 30 minutes.

4 Season with pepper to taste before serving.

	CALORIES	PROTEIN	FAT	CARBOHYDRATE	DIETARY FIBER	CALCIUM	SODIUM
per serving	364	7g	2g	88g	5g	85mg	17mg

Spicy Jicama Salad

spicy **JICAMA SALAD**

Jicama is a root vegetable indigenous to Mexico. Once the light-brown skin is removed, its white color, sweet flavor, and crunchy texture can be readily enjoyed. Increase or decrease the chile powder in this salad depending on how spicy you like your food.

4 cups sliced jicama (in 2 x ½-inch sticks)

4 oranges, peeled and sliced

2 cucumbers, sliced

¼ cup lime juice

¼ teaspoon chile powder or red chile flakes

1 Put all the ingredients in a large bowl.

2 Stir gently to combine, taking care not to break the orange slices too much.

3 Serve chilled or at room temperature.

	CALORIES	PROTEIN	FAT	CARBOHYDRATE	DIETARY FIBER	CALCIUM	SODIUM
per serving	**158**	**4**g	**1**g	**39**g	**11**g	**114**mg	**12**mg

radicchio and
PERSIMMON SALAD

T he bitter flavor of radicchio pairs very well with the sweetness of persimmon. Be sure to use only fuyu persimmons (which are round like a tomato) in this salad and not hachiya persimmons (which are acorn shaped). Hachiya persimmons have a very astringent flavor if they aren't fully ripe.

1 head radicchio, shredded

4 fuyu persimmons, sliced (peeling is optional)

4 stalks celery, chopped into 1-inch pieces

1 cup whole fresh mint leaves, lightly packed, coarsely chopped

Juice of 2 lemons

1 Put all the ingredients in a medium bowl.

2 Stir until well combined. Serve immediately.

	CALORIES	PROTEIN	FAT	CARBOHYDRATE	DIETARY FIBER	CALCIUM	SODIUM
per serving	145	2g	0g	38g	7g	33mg	26mg

grilled hearts
OF PALM SALAD

earts of palm are ivory colored and similar in texture to bamboo shoots. They are usually about one inch in diameter and three inches long. Look for them in the canned vegetable section of your supermarket. Make sure you rinse them well after opening the can in order to remove excess salt.

2 cans (14 ounces each) hearts of palm, **equal to 1 pound drained weight**

16 asparagus spears

2 cups unsalted cooked or canned white beans, **drained**

1 small red onion, **sliced into rings**

½ cup Lemon-Parsley Dressing (page 57)

1 Grill the hearts of palm and asparagus on a hot grill for 3–4 minutes per side.
2 Transfer to a large bowl and let cool.
3 Add the beans, onion, and dressing and stir until well combined. Serve chilled or at room temperature.

	CALORIES	PROTEIN	FAT	CARBOHYDRATE	DIETARY FIBER	CALCIUM	SODIUM
per serving	**183**	**13**g	**1**g	**32**g	**10**g	**148**mg	**426**mg

curried apples
AND WATERCRESS SALAD

T his salad can be made with the apples hot out of the oven or after they have cooled down a bit. The hot apples will have more flavor, but the salad will need to be served right away or the heat will wilt the watercress too much.

6 apples, peeled and cut into wedges

2 tablespoons curry powder

4 bunches watercress (about 4 cups), root ends cut off

2 cups cubed pineapple

1 small red onion, julienned

1 tablespoon rice vinegar

1 Preheat the oven to 400 degrees F.

2 Put the apples in a large bowl, add the curry powder, and stir until evenly distributed.

3 Arrange the apples in a single layer on a baking sheet and bake for 15 minutes.

4 Put the apples back in the large bowl. Add the watercress, pineapple, onion, and vinegar and stir until well combined. Serve immediately.

	CALORIES	PROTEIN	FAT	CARBOHYDRATE	DIETARY FIBER	CALCIUM	SODIUM
per serving	242	3g	1g	61g	11g	42mg	28mg

sweet winter
SQUASH SLAW

M y inspiration for this slaw comes from the traditional Thai green papaya salad, which typically contains fish sauce in the dressing. The naturally salty flavor of kale combined with lime and ginger comes close to replicating that flavor. The raw squash in this slaw adds a delightful contrast in texture and color.

1 small winter squash (such as butternut or kabocha)

4 cups chopped kale, firmly packed

½ cup peeled and chopped fresh ginger

Zest and juice of 2 large limes

½ cup chopped fresh cilantro, lightly packed

½ cup hazelnuts, toasted (see page 16) and slightly crushed

1 Using a sharp knife, carefully cut the squash in half and remove the seeds.

2 Cut the squash into manageable pieces and slice off the skin.

3 Put the squash through a food processor with a shredding attachment or use a box grater to shred it. Transfer to a large bowl.

4 Add the kale, ginger, lime zest and juice, and cilantro and stir until well combined.

5 Add the hazelnuts and stir until evenly distributed.

	CALORIES	PROTEIN	FAT	CARBOHYDRATE	DIETARY FIBER	CALCIUM	SODIUM
per serving	189	6g	10g	22g	6g	161mg	33mg

edamame
AND KALE SALAD

Edamame *are immature green soybeans that are cooked in the pod. You can find them shelled in the frozen-food section of most supermarkets, although some stores sell them still in the pod. In that case, you'll just have to manually shell them.*

4 cups shredded kale, lightly packed

2 cups frozen edamame

2 cups diced red bell pepper

2 tablespoons peeled and chopped fresh ginger

1 cup Mango-Ginger Dressing (page 51)

1 Put the kale, edamame, bell pepper, and ginger in a large bowl and stir until well combined.

2 Add the dressing and stir until evenly distributed. Serve chilled or at room temperature.

	CALORIES	PROTEIN	FAT	CARBOHYDRATE	DIETARY FIBER	CALCIUM	SODIUM
per serving	186	9g	4g	33g	5g	169mg	38mg

Edamame and Kale Salad

Salad DRESSINGS 3

A dressing can make or break a salad and be the deciding factor in whether someone will eat it. Therefore, a good dressing should pack a big flavor punch. There are three keys to a successful dressing:

1. A bold, predominant flavor.

2. The right viscosity. To give volume to a dressing, fruit juice or no-salt-added vegetable broth can be used instead of oil. Using the proper amount of one of these liquids based on the other ingredients in the dressing is what will provide the right viscosity.

3. An ingredient to help balance the predominant flavor. Having a little bit of a contrasting flavor is necessary to make the predominant flavor pop.

The dressings in this book are not only great on salads but also on steamed vegetables and grains. They're delicious cold, but don't be surprised if you like them warmed up too.

mango-ginger DRESSING

 A ripe mango will have a sweet fragrance before it's cut.

2 ripe mangoes

1 cup unsweetened apple juice

2 tablespoons peeled and chopped fresh ginger

1 teaspoon rice vinegar

1 tablespoon sesame seeds, toasted (see page 16)

1 Put the mangoes, apple juice, ginger, and vinegar in a blender.

2 Process on high speed until smooth.

3 Stir in the sesame seeds until evenly distributed.

	CALORIES	PROTEIN	FAT	CARBOHYDRATE	DIETARY FIBER	CALCIUM	SODIUM
per serving	97	1g	1g	22g	2g	30mg	3mg

orange-sesame
DRESSING

MAKES 2 CUPS, 8 SERVINGS

 he nutty taste of toasted sesame seeds combines with the sweet-and-sour taste of orange juice to give this dressing a perfectly balanced flavor.

1½ cups orange juice

6 tablespoons sesame seeds, toasted (see page 16)

1 shallot, chopped

1 Put all the ingredients in a blender.

2 Process on high speed until smooth.

	CALORIES	PROTEIN	FAT	CARBOHYDRATE	DIETARY FIBER	CALCIUM	SODIUM
per serving	62	2g	3g	7g	1g	68mg	2mg

52   CHAPTER 3

strawberry
BALSAMIC DRESSING

 he burgundy-red color of this dressing along with its playful sweet-and-sour profile will give any salad great visual contrast and flavor.

1½ cups strawberries, hulled

1 shallot, chopped

3 tablespoons balsamic vinegar

5 black peppercorns (optional)

1 Put all the ingredients in a blender.

2 Process on high speed until smooth.

	CALORIES	PROTEIN	FAT	CARBOHYDRATE	DIETARY FIBER	CALCIUM	SODIUM
per serving	23	0g	0g	5g	1g	10mg	3mg

datey mustard
DRESSING

MAKES 4 CUPS, 12 SERVINGS

*T*his is a wonderful alternative to the ever-popular honey-mustard dressing, because on a vegan diet, honey is a no-no. But don't worry, the datey flavor in this recipe replaces the honey without missing a beat. For a well-rounded mustard flavor, try using a combination of stone-ground and yellow mustard.

2 cups water

8 pitted dates, chopped

1 cup mustard (choose your favorite kind)

1 recipe Roasted Parsnips and Shallots (page 96)

1 Put the water and dates in a small pot and cook over low heat, stirring occasionally, for 20 minutes.

2 Strain out and discard the dates but save the liquid.

3 When the date water is cool, pour it into a blender.

4 Add the mustard and Roasted Parsnips and Shallots and process on high speed until smooth.

	CALORIES	PROTEIN	FAT	CARBOHYDRATE	DIETARY FIBER	CALCIUM	SODIUM
per serving	76	1g	0g	15g	3g	31mg	207mg

roasted garlic
DRESSING

f you like toasty flavors, you'll love this dressing. Roasted garlic has a mellow, sweet flavor compared to the intense and overwhelming taste of raw garlic.

1¼ cups no-salt-added vegetable broth

¾ cup garlic cloves, roasted (see page 15)

½ ripe avocado

¼ cup sunflower seeds, toasted (see page 16)

Juice of 1 lime

1 Put all the ingredients in a blender.

2 Process on high speed until smooth.

	CALORIES	PROTEIN	FAT	CARBOHYDRATE	DIETARY FIBER	CALCIUM	SODIUM
per serving	64	1g	3g	8g	2g	34mg	4mg

kel-pea DRESSING

MAKES 3 CUPS, 9 SERVINGS

I was trying to come up with a healthy alternative to green goddess dressing, and kelp powder seemed like the perfect replacement for oily, salty anchovies. It has a dark forest-green color and a naturally salty taste.

1 cup frozen green peas, thawed

1 cup no-salt-added vegetable broth

¼ cup raw cashews

Juice of 1 lemon

1 tablespoon kelp powder

1 tablespoon stone-ground mustard

1 Put all the ingredients in a blender.

2 Process on high speed until smooth.

	CALORIES	PROTEIN	FAT	CARBOHYDRATE	DIETARY FIBER	CALCIUM	SODIUM
per serving	38	2g	2g	4g	1g	7mg	17mg

lemon-parsley
DRESSING

Lemon and parsley is a flavor combination that's been enjoyed for ages. This recipe gives you a chance to use it in a delicious new way.

1 cup lemon juice

1 cup chopped fresh parsley, lightly packed

¼ cup raw cashews

5 garlic cloves

1 Put all the ingredients in a blender.

2 Process on high speed until smooth.

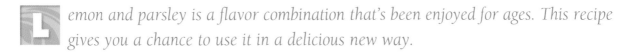

	CALORIES	PROTEIN	FAT	CARBOHYDRATE	DIETARY FIBER	CALCIUM	SODIUM
per serving	45	2g	3g	5g	1g	31mg	7mg

tomatillo **DRESSING**

MAKES 2 CUPS, 6 SERVINGS

 hen you're working with tomatillos, start by removing their husks and then giving them a good rinse to remove their sticky residue.

2 cups chopped tomatillos

½ cup chopped green onions, lightly packed

½ ripe avocado

½ cup chopped fresh cilantro, lightly packed

½ cup no-salt-added vegetable broth

2 garlic cloves

¼ teaspoon ground cumin (optional)

1 Put all the ingredients in a blender.

2 Process on high speed until smooth.

	CALORIES	PROTEIN	FAT	CARBOHYDRATE	DIETARY FIBER	CALCIUM	SODIUM
per serving	57	1g	4g	5g	2g	15mg	12mg

smoky tomato
DRESSING

A nyone who loves smoky flavor and wants to incorporate it into a healthy diet will appreciate this recipe. When tomatoes get blended, they lose some of their color. The smoked paprika helps intensify the red color and also adds a hint of smoke that pairs beautifully with the sweet-tart flavor of the tomatoes.

8 Roma tomatoes, cut in half lengthwise

2 yellow onions, sliced

8 garlic cloves

4 teaspoons smoked paprika

No-salt-added vegetable broth, as needed

1 Preheat the oven to 350 degrees F. Line a baking sheet with parchment paper or a silicone baking mat.

2 Put the tomatoes, onions, and garlic on the prepared baking sheet in a single layer.

3 Roast in the oven for 25–30 minutes. Remove from the oven and let cool.

4 Put the tomatoes, onions, garlic, and smoked paprika in a blender. Process on high speed until smooth, adding broth as needed to achieve the desired consistency.

	CALORIES	PROTEIN	FAT	CARBOHYDRATE	DIETARY FIBER	CALCIUM	SODIUM
per serving	21	1g	0g	5g	1g	11mg	5mg

jalapeño-peanut
DRESSING

*I*t's hard to predict how spicy jalapeño chiles will be, so put in just half to start with and then taste the dressing so you can decide whether it has enough heat or you want more.

1 jalapeño chile, cut in half, with seeds

1 cup no-salt-added vegetable broth

¼ cup rice vinegar

¼ cup raw peanuts, toasted (see page 16)

1 Put all the ingredients in a blender.

2 Process on high speed for 1 minute.

	CALORIES	PROTEIN	FAT	CARBOHYDRATE	DIETARY FIBER	CALCIUM	SODIUM
per serving	33	1g	2g	1g	0g	4mg	18mg

Starch and
STARCH-ISH 4

So let me get this straight. Starches, such as potatoes, yams, rice, and corn, are staple foods that have sustained many cultures and countries for hundreds, maybe thousands, of years, but suddenly they are bad for you? Give me a break!

Whole-food starches offer many advantages. First, they fill you up quickly without contributing too many calories to your diet. For example, one pound of cooked potatoes is about 400 calories, and one cup cooked brown rice is about 500 calories. In comparison, one pound of bread is about 1,200 calories—three times as many calories as potatoes. Second, a whole-foods plant-based diet that's centered around starches is fairly inexpensive, especially if you purchase grains such as rice and polenta in bulk and store them for a while. Third, and most important as far as I'm concerned, is that these foods are so versatile. They can be eaten hot or cold, as a main dish or side dish, and can be cooked in a variety of ways. In fact, when it comes to eating whole-food starches, there are nothing but pluses.

Cilantro-Buttered Corn

cilantro-buttered CORN

The cilantro butter for this recipe is brimming with flavor. It provides a healthier alternative to the ever-popular buttery, cheesy, salty way of flavoring corn on the cob.

1 cup no-salt-added vegetable broth

4 ears of corn

½ cup chopped fresh cilantro, lightly packed

¼ cup raw cashews, toasted (see page 16)

Pinch cayenne (optional)

1. Put ¾ cup of the broth in a large pot. Cover and bring to a boil over high heat.

2. Add the corn, cover, decrease the heat to medium, and cook until the broth has evaporated, about 5 minutes.

3. To make the cilantro butter, put the cilantro, cashews, and remaining ¼ cup of broth in a small food processor or small blender and process for 1 minute.

4. Smear each ear of corn with the cilantro butter and sprinkle with cayenne if desired.

	CALORIES	PROTEIN	FAT	CARBOHYDRATE	DIETARY FIBER	CALCIUM	SODIUM
per serving	183	6g	6g	32g	5g	4mg	25mg

herbed POTATOES

U sing two different-colored potatoes in this recipe provides an eye-appealing contrast. Of course, you can just use one type of potato. The dish won't be as pretty, but it will still taste good.

2 pounds small yellow potatoes, cut in half

2 pounds small purple potatoes, cut in half

1 teaspoon chopped fresh tarragon

1 teaspoon chopped fresh thyme

1 Steam the yellow and purple potatoes until tender. Make sure the potatoes don't sit in the water while cooking and that the water doesn't evaporate before the potatoes are done.

2 Transfer the potatoes to a large bowl. Add the tarragon and thyme and stir gently until evenly distributed.

	CALORIES	PROTEIN	FAT	CARBOHYDRATE	DIETARY FIBER	CALCIUM	SODIUM
per serving	313	8g	1g	71g	11g	41mg	27mg

oven-roasted
PLANTAIN FAJITAS

P lantains are in the banana family, but they are larger than regular bananas. Their starch content is much higher too, which is why they are seldom eaten raw and are usually baked, roasted, or fried. Plantains are ripe when they're half black and half yellow. You can find fresh epazote in most Latin supermarkets.

4 ripe plantains

2 cups sliced red onions

2 cups sliced green bell peppers

Juice of 1 lime

1 teaspoon chopped fresh epazote, cilantro, or basil

1 Preheat the oven to 350 degrees F.

2 Put the plantains on a baking sheet and bake for 15 minutes, or until the skins burst open.

3 Dry sauté the onions, peppers, lime juice, and epazote in a large skillet over medium heat for 2–3 minutes.

4 To serve, spoon some of the onions and peppers over the middle of each plantain.

	CALORIES	PROTEIN	FAT	CARBOHYDRATE	DIETARY FIBER	CALCIUM	SODIUM
per serving	268	4g	1g	69g	7g	39mg	12mg

buckwheat
TABBOULEH

 lthough its name is a little misleading, buckwheat is actually a seed, not a grain.

4 cups cooked buckwheat (see page 19)

2 Roma tomatoes, seeded and diced

2 small cucumbers, peeled and sliced

1 cup chopped fresh parsley, lightly packed

Zest and juice of 2 large lemons

½ cup chopped pistachios, roasted (see page 16)

Freshly ground black pepper

1 Put the buckwheat, tomatoes, cucumbers, parsley, lemon zest and juice, and pistachios in a large bowl. Stir until well combined.

2 Season with pepper to taste.

	CALORIES	PROTEIN	FAT	CARBOHYDRATE	DIETARY FIBER	CALCIUM	SODIUM
per serving	224	9g	5g	43g	8g	64mg	19mg

Buckwheat Tabbouleh

yam FRIES

 ither yams or sweet potatoes will work well for this recipe, but if you use one of each, the dish will have a beautiful contrast of colors.

2 large yams, cut into ½-inch-thick strips

1 teaspoon granulated garlic

Mustard, for serving

1 Preheat the oven to 400 degrees F. Line a baking sheet with parchment paper or a silicone baking mat.

2 Arrange the yam strips in a single layer on the prepared baking sheet and sprinkle them with the garlic. Bake for 15–20 minutes, depending on how browned you like your fries. Rotate the baking sheet midway in the cooking cycle for even browning.

3 Serve with mustard on the side for dipping.

	CALORIES	PROTEIN	FAT	CARBOHYDRATE	DIETARY FIBER	CALCIUM	SODIUM
per serving	167	4g	0g	39g	6g	7mg	65mg

roasted-garlic
MASHED POTATOES

The secret to fluffy mashed potatoes is mixing them as soon as they're done steaming. If they're allowed to cool down, they'll become gummy. If you really love garlic, double up on the roasted garlic cloves.

8 Yukon gold potatoes, peeled and cut in half

1 cup unsweetened soy milk, heated

¼ cup garlic cloves, roasted (see page 15)

1 Steam the potatoes until very tender, about 30 minutes. Make sure the potatoes don't sit in the water while cooking and that the water doesn't evaporate before the potatoes are done. Transfer to a medium bowl.

2 Put the hot soy milk and garlic in a blender and process on high speed for 20 seconds. Pour over the hot potatoes and mash until well combined.

	CALORIES	PROTEIN	FAT	CARBOHYDRATE	DIETARY FIBER	CALCIUM	SODIUM
per serving	310	8g	2g	68g	7g	37mg	24mg

Spicy Soba Noodles

spicy
SOBA NOODLES

Soba noodles work well in this recipe because they cook quickly, but any type of noodle can be substituted if you prefer.

6 ounces soba noodles

2 cups Jalapeño-Peanut Dressing (page 60)

1 cup shredded carrots

1 cup fresh basil leaves, **lightly packed**

¼ cup peeled and chopped fresh ginger

1 teaspoon sesame seeds, **toasted** (see page 16; optional)

1 Cook the noodles according to the package instructions. Drain in a colander and rinse under cold water.

2 Transfer the noodles to a medium bowl. Add the dressing, carrots, basil, ginger, and optional sesame seeds and stir gently until well combined.

	CALORIES	PROTEIN	FAT	CARBOHYDRATE	DIETARY FIBER	CALCIUM	SODIUM
per serving	**229**	**9**g	**5**g	**38**g	**2**g	**51**mg	**345**mg

quinoa and
ARUGULA SALAD

 f you happen to have leftover quinoa in the fridge, this recipe is a great way to inject it with lots of flavor and moisture.

4 cups cooked quinoa (see page 19)

4 cups arugula, lightly packed

1 cup shredded carrots

1 cup fresh basil, lightly packed

1 cup orange juice

Freshly ground black pepper (optional)

1 Put the quinoa, arugula, carrots, basil, and orange juice in a large bowl and stir until well combined.

2 Season with pepper to taste if desired. Serve chilled or at room temperature.

	CALORIES	PROTEIN	FAT	CARBOHYDRATE	DIETARY FIBER	CALCIUM	SODIUM
per serving	223	8g	3g	43g	5g	43mg	58mg

banana and
FLAXSEED POLENTA

 his dish can be served hot as a breakfast item or as a dessert.

4 cups unsweetened apple juice

6 ripe bananas

1 cup coarsely ground cornmeal (polenta)

4 tablespoons ground flaxseeds

1 Put the apple juice and 3 of the bananas in a blender and process until smooth and thick.

2 Pour into a medium pot and bring to a boil over medium-high heat.

3 Stir in the cornmeal, decrease the heat to low, and cook, stirring occasionally, for 20 minutes.

4 Chop the remaining 3 bananas and add them to the pot along with the flaxseeds. Stir until well combined.

	CALORIES	PROTEIN	FAT	CARBOHYDRATE	DIETARY FIBER	CALCIUM	SODIUM
per serving	387	6g	6g	81g	9g	26mg	9mg

wild rice
AND SPINACH

 he wild rice for this recipe can be cooked a day or two in advance. If it's cooked the same day you'll be serving it, this salad will have a softer texture.

4 cups cooked wild rice (see page 19)

4 cups spinach leaves, lightly packed

2 cups diced celery

1 cup whole fresh mint leaves, lightly packed

½ cup lime juice

¼ cup walnuts, toasted (see page 16)

1 Put all the ingredients in a large bowl and stir until well combined.

2 Serve chilled or at room temperature.

	CALORIES	PROTEIN	FAT	CARBOHYDRATE	DIETARY FIBER	CALCIUM	SODIUM
per serving	231	9g	6g	39g	5g	67mg	70mg

Wild Rice and Spinach

Where Do You Get YOUR PROTEIN? 5

Vegans get asked this question quite a lot. That's why I decided to include a bean-inspired section in this book. But I'm going to let you in on a little secret. Anyone, and I mean *anyone*, regardless of their diet—paleo, vegan, pescaterian, vegetarian, or whatever else—would have to work really, really hard to be protein deficient. Why? Because most plant foods, including vegetables, such as kale and broccoli, have protein. Protein isn't exclusive to meat and beans. Popular fruits, such as oranges, kiwis, and bananas, also have protein. Quite frankly, chasing the right amount of protein in your diet is a waste of time. If you eat enough food to stay alive, you're more than likely getting enough protein.

So why do people focus on making sure they get enough protein? Because of the big ad campaigns enacted by the commercial food industry. When a food product's label touts the high amount of protein the item contains, the public thinks it's a healthy food, no questions asked. Our society as a whole generally believes that more is always better. But, again, you would have to work extremely hard to be protein deficient. So I encourage you not to fall for this silly propaganda that isn't based in science and simply targets your wallet. Instead, let me pose a much better question: Where do you get your fiber? Now that's a way more important question you should be asking if you really care about health. Fiber is essential for the absorption of nutrients during digestion. It also helps you poop regularly. Want to get in on another secret? Beans are a great source of fiber!

yellow
CURRY LENTILS

 entils are delicious and adaptable. If you cut the amount of broth in half, this stew can be transformed into a dip, which can then be served hot or cold.

2 cups sliced oyster or white button mushrooms

1 yellow onion, diced

2 tablespoons yellow curry powder

1 tablespoon chopped garlic

8 cups no-salt-added vegetable broth

2 cups yellow or red split lentils

2 cups baby arugula, lightly packed (optional)

1 Dry sauté the mushrooms, onion, curry powder, and garlic in a medium pot over medium heat for 3 minutes.

2 Add the broth and bring to a simmer.

3 Add the lentils and cook, stirring occasionally, until tender, about 20 minutes.

4 Stir in the arugula just before serving.

	CALORIES	PROTEIN	FAT	CARBOHYDRATE	DIETARY FIBER	CALCIUM	SODIUM
per serving	393	26g	1g	69g	26g	67mg	19mg

Cajun-roasted
NAVY BEANS AND MUSHROOMS

MAKES 4 SERVINGS

 There are hundreds of Cajun spice blends available, including some without salt. The right one to use is the one you like best.

8 cups quartered shiitake or oyster mushrooms

4 cups unsalted cooked or canned navy or garbanzo beans, drained

2 cups coarsely chopped green onions

1 cup no-salt-added vegetable broth

1 tablespoon Cajun spice blend

2 teaspoons red wine vinegar

1 Preheat the oven to 400 degrees F.

2 Put all the ingredients in a large baking dish and stir to combine. Bake for 10 minutes.

3 Stir and bake for 10 minutes longer. Serve hot or at room temperature.

	CALORIES	PROTEIN	FAT	CARBOHYDRATE	DIETARY FIBER	CALCIUM	SODIUM
per serving	325	20g	1g	62g	22g	162mg	8mg

Cajun-Roasted Navy Beans and Mushrooms

GARBANZO crunch

 hese addictively delicious morsels will squelch any cravings you might have for fried snacks.

6 cups unsalted cooked or canned garbanzo beans, drained

1 cup lime juice

1 teaspoon chili powder

1 teaspoon granulated garlic

1. Preheat the oven to 350 degrees F.

2. Spread the beans in a single layer on a baking sheet. Bake for 30 minutes.

3. Remove the beans from the oven. Keep the oven on but decrease the temperature to 200 degrees F.

4. Transfer the beans to a large bowl. Add the lime juice, chili powder, and garlic and stir to combine. Let marinate for 10 minutes.

5. Spread the beans in a single layer on the baking sheet and bake for 90 minutes, or until crunchy.

	CALORIES	PROTEIN	FAT	CARBOHYDRATE	DIETARY FIBER	CALCIUM	SODIUM
per serving	408	22g	7g	68g	19g	123mg	24mg

coriander-spiced
ROOTS AND PINTOS

Fenugreek seeds have a sweet aroma but a bitter taste. Once they're toasted, though, the bitterness virtually disappears.

6 cups unsalted cooked or canned pinto beans, drained

4 cups cubed turnips

4 cups cubed rutabaga

1 red onion, chopped

1 cup orange juice

1 tablespoon ground coriander, toasted (see page 16)

2 tablespoons chopped fresh chives (optional)

1 Preheat the oven to 350 degrees F.

2 Put the beans, turnips, rutabaga, onion, orange juice, and coriander in a large baking pan and stir to combine. Bake for 10 minutes.

3 Remove from the oven, stir, and bake for 10 minutes longer.

4 Garnish with the optional chives. Serve hot.

	CALORIES	PROTEIN	FAT	CARBOHYDRATE	DIETARY FIBER	CALCIUM	SODIUM
per serving	506	27g	2g	99g	30g	258mg	63mg

Caraway-Mustard Kidney Beans

caraway-mustard
KIDNEY BEANS

Sometimes naughty food can inspire healthy dishes. This one is based on the flavors of the traditional reuben sandwich. The key ingredients are caraway seeds, for their distinctive flavor; cabbage and mustard, which stand in for the sauerkraut; and kidney beans, for the reddish protein. The takeaway? You don't have to reinvent the wheel to create healthy food—you just have to point it in the right direction.

4 cups chopped savoy or green cabbage

2 cups chopped leeks (white and light-green parts only)

4 cups unsalted cooked or canned kidney beans, drained

2 cups no-salt-added vegetable broth

¼ cup mustard (choose your favorite kind)

¼ teaspoon whole caraway seeds, toasted (see page 16)

1 Dry sauté the cabbage and leeks in a large pot over medium-high heat, stirring frequently, for 3 minutes.

2 Add the kidney beans, broth, mustard, and caraway seeds and bring to a simmer.

3 Decrease the heat to low and cook until the liquid is almost gone, 8–10 minutes. Serve hot.

	CALORIES	PROTEIN	FAT	CARBOHYDRATE	DIETARY FIBER	CALCIUM	SODIUM
per serving	297	17g	1g	53g	16g	111mg	28mg

hearty balsamic
HUMMUS

Balsamic vinegar isn't an ingredient that's traditional in hummus, but it adds an extra bit of zing. Serve this hummus as a dip for veggie sticks or pita bread, or use it as a topping for baked potatoes or rice cakes.

4 cups unsalted cooked or canned garbanzo beans, drained

½ cup balsamic vinegar

Juice of 1 lemon

2 tablespoons sesame seeds, toasted (see page 16)

2 garlic cloves

1 teaspoon crushed red pepper flakes

1 Put all the ingredients in a food processor.

2 Process until the desired consistency is achieved.

	CALORIES	PROTEIN	FAT	CARBOHYDRATE	DIETARY FIBER	CALCIUM	SODIUM
per serving	333	16g	7g	54g	14g	134mg	20mg

Indian-spiced
BAKED BEANS

S *pices benefit greatly by being toasted prior to cooking with them in order to bring out their flavor and aroma. Whole spices will almost always have more flavor if you grind them yourself than if you purchase them already ground.*

1 teaspoon coriander seeds, toasted (see page 16)

1 teaspoon cumin seeds, toasted (see page 16)

1 teaspoon mustard seeds, toasted (see page 16)

8 cups unsalted cooked or canned black beans, drained

2 cups chopped canned or packaged tomatoes

½ teaspoon ground turmeric, toasted (see page 16)

¼ cup chopped fresh cilantro, lightly packed (optional)

1 Preheat the oven to 350 degrees F.

2 Coarsely grind the coriander, cumin, and mustard seeds in a spice grinder for 2–3 seconds. Alternatively, put them on a cutting board and press down on them with a heavy pot or pan to crush them.

3 Put the beans, tomatoes, coriander, cumin, mustard seeds, and turmeric in a large baking dish and stir until well combined. Bake for 10 minutes.

4 Remove from the oven, stir, and bake for 10 minutes longer.

5 Garnish with the optional cilantro. Serve hot.

	CALORIES	PROTEIN	FAT	CARBOHYDRATE	DIETARY FIBER	CALCIUM	SODIUM
per serving	483	32g	3g	87g	32g	143mg	17mg

CREAMY tofu

The firmness of the tofu used for this recipe will affect the texture of this dish. One isn't better than the other, though; it's just personal preference. The softer the tofu, the creamier the end result will be, so go with what you like best. Think of it as the difference between creamy versus crunchy peanut butter. Use this savory topping as a spread for whole-grain bread or crackers or as a replacement for sour cream on baked or steamed potatoes and yams.

1 package (14 ounces) firm or extra-firm tofu

1½ cups chopped green onions, lightly packed

1 cup Kel-Pea Dressing (page 56)

½ teaspoon ground turmeric

Freshly ground black pepper

1 Put the tofu, green onions, dressing, and turmeric in a food processor. Pulse just until evenly distributed, 8–10 seconds.

2 Season with pepper to taste.

3 Cover and chill in the refrigerator for at least 1 hour before serving. Serve cold.

	CALORIES	PROTEIN	FAT	CARBOHYDRATE	DIETARY FIBER	CALCIUM	SODIUM
per serving	121	11g	6g	8g	2g	209mg	40mg

Vegetable DISHES

6

Although veggie dishes are usually considered enhancements to the main dish, when you eat a healthy diet, they can be the central attraction. They are faster and simpler to make than entrees, which means you can cook and eat several of them and thereby have a wider variety when you sit down for a meal. They're also great toppers for plain starches, such as steamed rice, potatoes, or quinoa, and add color and texture to many dishes. Have you heard the saying "eat the rainbow"? This is where you make it happen, as vegetables come in a dazzling array of hues.

ORANGE-BRAISED fennel

 ennel is one of the most versatile vegetables around. From raw to roasted and everything in between, fennel can delight your palate in many different ways.

4 oranges

2 medium fennel bulbs, quartered

2 stalks celery, diced large

2 shallots, diced large

Fennel tops (optional)

1 Remove the zest from two of the oranges, then juice all of the oranges.

2 Dry sauté the fennel, celery, and shallots in a large sauté pan over medium-high heat, stirring frequently, until nicely browned, about 5 minutes.

3 Add the orange zest and juice, decrease the heat to low, cover, and cook until only a small amount of liquid is left in the pan, about 2 minutes.

4 Garnish with fennel tops if desired. Serve hot.

	CALORIES	PROTEIN	FAT	CARBOHYDRATE	DIETARY FIBER	CALCIUM	SODIUM
per serving	124	4g	0g	31g	8g	88mg	113mg

sherry-roasted **PEARLS**

Sherry vinegar has a bold yet elegant and smooth flavor and aroma. It tends to be less acidic than other vinegars, so more can be used in cooking without overwhelming the palate.

2 cups pearl onions, **root ends cut off**

1 pound baby carrots, **peeled**

¼ cup no-salt-added vegetable broth

2 tablespoons sherry vinegar

1 teaspoon chopped fresh thyme

1 Fill a medium pot halfway with water and bring to a boil over medium-high heat. Add the onions and cook for 1 minute.

2 Dump the onions into a strainer and let cool until they can be easily handled.

3 Squeeze the onions from the top so they will pop out of their skins. Discard the skins.

4 Put the empty pot back on the stove, and preheat it over medium-high heat for 1 minute.

5 Put the onions and carrots in the pot and cook, stirring frequently, until well browned, 3–4 minutes.

6 Add the broth, vinegar, and thyme, cover, and cook for 1 minute. Serve hot.

	CALORIES	PROTEIN	FAT	CARBOHYDRATE	DIETARY FIBER	CALCIUM	SODIUM
per serving	190	5g	0g	43g	10g	104mg	264mg

baby bok choy
AND MACADAMIAS

Baby bok choy doesn't grow up to be regular bok choy; these are actually two different vegetables. However, you can substitute one for the other. The flavor of baby bok choy is just a tad milder than its big brother, and its leaves are more tender.

2 shallots, sliced thick

6 baby bok choy, cut into quarters

Juice of 2 tangerines

½ cup chopped fresh basil, lightly packed

8 macadamia nuts, toasted (see page 16) and crushed in half

1　Dry sauté the shallots in a large skillet over medium-high heat, stirring frequently, for 1 minute.

2　Add the baby bok choy and tangerine juice, cover, and cook for 1 minute.

3　Stir in the basil and macadamia nuts. Serve immediately.

	CALORIES	PROTEIN	FAT	CARBOHYDRATE	DIETARY FIBER	CALCIUM	SODIUM
per serving	95	3g	5g	13g	3g	142mg	16mg

cider-steamed
SWISS CHARD

 he sweetness of the apple cider juxtaposed with the saltiness of the Swiss chard makes this dish phenomenal.

1 cup sliced red onion

1 tablespoon chopped garlic

8 cups chopped Swiss chard (any color), lightly packed

¼ cup apple cider

Freshly ground black pepper

1 Dry sauté the onion and garlic in a large pot over high heat, stirring frequently, for 2 minutes.

2 Add the Swiss chard and cook, stirring constantly, for 30 seconds.

3 Add the cider, cover, and cook for 2 minutes.

4 Season with pepper to taste. Serve hot.

	CALORIES	PROTEIN	FAT	CARBOHYDRATE	DIETARY FIBER	CALCIUM	SODIUM
per serving	94	2g	0g	22g	2g	51mg	186mg

brussels sprouts
AND DRIED FIGS

*L*ike all dried fruit, dried figs are not only sweet but sturdy. So if you don't have dried figs available and need a replacement, choose another dried fruit, such as apricots or peaches. Be advised, if you attempt this recipe with fresh figs or other fresh fruit, the outcome will be a mushy mess.

4 cups Brussels sprouts, cut in half

1 cup sliced red onion

½ cup chopped dried figs

½ cup no-salt-added vegetable broth

Zest and juice of 2 lemons

1 tablespoon chopped fresh sage

1 Dry sauté the Brussels sprouts, onion, and figs in a medium pot over medium-high heat, stirring frequently, just until they begin to brown, 3–4 minutes.

2 Add the broth and lemon zest and juice, cover, and cook for 5 minutes.

3 Stir in the sage just before serving. Serve hot.

	CALORIES	PROTEIN	FAT	CARBOHYDRATE	DIETARY FIBER	CALCIUM	SODIUM
per serving	120	5g	1g	28g	7g	84mg	36mg

braised red cabbage
WITH DRIED CHERRIES

 he dish is evocative of sauerkraut but with a sweet touch from the cherries.

2 red cabbages, shredded

2 cups diced leeks (white and light-green parts only)

2 cups diced celery

½ cup unsweetened dried cherries

1½ cups apple cider vinegar

2 tablespoons chopped fresh thyme

1 Put the cabbage, leeks, celery, and cherries in a large pot. Cook over medium heat, stirring frequently, for 10 minutes.

2 Add the vinegar, decrease the heat to medium-low, cover, and cook, stirring occasionally, for 30 minutes.

3 Uncover and cook, stirring occasionally, for 10 minutes longer, or until the cabbage is dry.

4 Add the thyme and stir until evenly distributed. Serve hot.

	CALORIES	PROTEIN	FAT	CARBOHYDRATE	DIETARY FIBER	CALCIUM	SODIUM
per serving	156	4g	0g	38g	7g	151mg	114mg

lemon-garlic
BROCCOLINI

 Broccolini, *also known as baby broccoli, has a slight chestnut flavor that adds depth to this recipe.*

2 tablespoons sliced garlic

1 pound broccolini or broccoli rabe

¼ cup no-salt-added vegetable broth

Zest and juice of 1 lemon

1 tablespoon chopped green onions

1 Dry sauté the garlic in a medium sauté pan over medium heat for 1 minute.

2 Add the broccolini and cook, stirring frequently, for 1 minute.

3 Add the broth and lemon zest and juice, cover, and cook for 2 minutes.

4 Garnish with the green onions. Serve hot.

	CALORIES	PROTEIN	FAT	CARBOHYDRATE	DIETARY FIBER	CALCIUM	SODIUM
per serving	117	9g	0g	22g	4g	184mg	79mg

Lemon-Garlic Broccolini

roasted parsnips
AND SHALLOTS

Parsnips *look like big whitish carrots. However, they are more savory than sweet.*

6 cups peeled and coarsely chopped parsnips

6 shallots, quartered

½ cup no-salt-added vegetable broth

1 tablespoon chopped fresh thyme

1 Preheat the oven to 350 degrees F.

2 Put the parsnips, shallots, and broth in a medium baking pan and cover with aluminum foil. Bake for 45 minutes.

3 Remove from the oven and stir in the thyme. Serve hot.

	CALORIES	PROTEIN	FAT	CARBOHYDRATE	DIETARY FIBER	CALCIUM	SODIUM
per serving	155	3g	0g	35g	8g	79mg	22mg

roasted **CACTUS FINGERS**

 actus leaves can be found in most Latin supermarkets. Many times you can find them peeled (the thorns cut off). They're a bit more expensive but worth it.

8 cactus leaves

2 red onions, cut into thick rounds

4 Roma tomatoes, cut in half

12 garlic cloves

Juice of 2 limes

1 teaspoon ground cumin

1 Preheat the oven to 400 degrees F. Line a baking sheet with parchment paper or a silicone baking mat.

2 Make three or four cuts in each cactus leaf, starting from the two-thirds mark through the thicker end. Each cactus leaf should look like a hand with fingers still attached.

3 Put the cactus leaves, onions, tomatoes, garlic, lime juice, and cumin in a large bowl and stir to combine.

4 Spread into a single layer on the lined baking sheet and roast for 15 minutes.

5 Stir, spread into a single layer again, and roast for 5 minutes longer. Serve hot or cold.

	CALORIES	PROTEIN	FAT	CARBOHYDRATE	DIETARY FIBER	CALCIUM	SODIUM
per serving	106	4g	1g	25g	5g	225mg	29mg

ginger-steamed EGGPLANT

Although regular eggplant can be used in this dish, it must be peeled, as its skin tends to be bitter, whereas the skin of Japanese eggplant (which is similar in size and shape to a large zucchini) is not.

4 large Japanese eggplants

½ cup peeled and chopped fresh ginger

¾ cup no-salt-added vegetable broth

1 Preheat the oven to 350 degrees F.

2 Slice the eggplants into one-half-inch-thick rounds. Arrange the rounds in a single layer in a baking dish, sprinkle with the ginger, and pour the broth over them.

3 Cover the dish with foil and bake for 30 minutes, or until soft. Serve hot.

CHEF'S TIP: To test if the eggplant is fully cooked, you should be able to poke a hole in it with your finger.

	CALORIES	PROTEIN	FAT	CARBOHYDRATE	DIETARY FIBER	CALCIUM	SODIUM
per serving	60	2g	0g	12g	4g	2mg	3mg

RAJAS

Rajas *means "strips" or "slices" in Spanish. In the culinary sense, it refers to a dish of sliced poblano chiles and onions with sour cream. In this healthy version of rajas, a blend of spicy, sweet, and sour flavors comes together to enhance the chiles.*

4 cups julienned poblano chiles

4 cups julienned red onions

2 cups cherry tomatoes, cut in half

Juice of 2 limes

½ cup chopped fresh cilantro, lightly packed

1 Dry sauté the chiles and onions in a large pot over medium-high heat, stirring occasionally, until they begin to brown.

2 Add the tomatoes, lime juice, and cilantro and cook, stirring constantly, for 30 seconds. Serve hot.

	CALORIES	PROTEIN	FAT	CARBOHYDRATE	DIETARY FIBER	CALCIUM	SODIUM
per serving	121	3g	1g	29g	5g	76mg	17mg

Pan-Roasted Zucchini and Carrot Balls

pan-roasted zucchini
AND CARROT BALLS

A melon baller is needed for this recipe in order to make the zucchini and carrot balls. Yes, it's a bit wasteful, but the dish has a wonderful and unique visual effect. To scoop out the balls, insert the melon baller into the flesh of the vegetables and twist it 180 degrees, as if you were scooping a ball of ice cream.

1 cup zucchini balls

1 cup carrot balls

1 shallot, chopped

½ teaspoon ground cumin

Zest and juice of 1 lemon

1 Preheat a medium sauté pan over medium-high heat for 3 minutes.

2 Add the zucchini and carrot balls and cook, stirring frequently, until they begin to brown.

3 Add the shallot and cumin and cook, stirring constantly, for 30 seconds.

4 Add the lemon zest and juice and stir until the liquid evaporates, about 1 minute. Serve immediately.

	CALORIES	PROTEIN	FAT	CARBOHYDRATE	DIETARY FIBER	CALCIUM	SODIUM
per serving	59	2g	0g	15g	3g	43mg	53mg

oven-roasted
RED KURI SQUASH

Red kuri squash has a bright-orange skin, similar to pumpkin but without the ridges, and is very sweet. Its best feature is that it doesn't need to be peeled because its skin doesn't change the flavor or texture of a dish. You can replace the red kuri squash with kabocha or butternut squash, but the skin will need to be removed.

1 medium red kuri squash, cut into wedges, seeds removed

½ green cabbage, sliced medium

½ red cabbage, sliced medium

2 cups Pecan Gremolata (page 125)

1. Preheat the oven to 350 degrees F. Line a baking sheet with parchment paper or a silicone baking mat.

2. Arrange the squash in a single layer on the lined baking sheet. Bake for 15 minutes.

3. Arrange the cabbage on top of the squash. Bake for 15 minutes. Let the vegetables cool until they can be easily handled.

4. Add the gremolata and mix until evenly distributed. Serve immediately.

	CALORIES	PROTEIN	FAT	CARBOHYDRATE	DIETARY FIBER	CALCIUM	SODIUM
per serving	175	6g	6g	30g	7g	172mg	62mg

steamed asparagus
AND ARTICHOKE HEARTS

F or a nicer presentation and mouthfeel, peel the asparagus. This will remove the chewy, fibrous skin, leaving the asparagus soft and tender. It's important to serve this dish as soon as it's finished cooking; otherwise, the asparagus will turn a funky green color.

½ cup sliced red onion

1 garlic clove, sliced thin

20 asparagus, bottoms trimmed

1 cup canned (packed in water) or thawed frozen artichoke hearts

Zest and juice of 1 orange

Freshly ground black pepper

1 Dry sauté the onion and garlic in a medium sauté pan over medium-high heat for 2 minutes.

2 Add the asparagus and artichokes and cook for 1 minute.

3 Add the orange zest and juice, cover, and cook for 1 minute.

4 Season with pepper to taste. Serve immediately.

	CALORIES	PROTEIN	FAT	CARBOHYDRATE	DIETARY FIBER	CALCIUM	SODIUM
per serving	141	8g	0g	29g	9g	130mg	386mg

roasted cauliflower
AND PEAS

The mustard is optional in this recipe, as it's great with or without it. Roasted cauliflower has a rich, complex flavor, but it's a bit dry. The mustard offsets that by adding moisture, but it masks the other flavors a bit. I'll leave it up to you to decide which way to go.

1 large cauliflower, cut into small florets

2 shallots, chopped

2 cups frozen peas, thawed

2 tablespoons chopped fresh basil

1 tablespoon stone-ground mustard (optional)

1 Preheat the oven to 400 degrees F. Line a baking sheet with parchment paper.

2 Arrange the cauliflower and shallots in a single layer on the lined baking sheet. Bake for 10 minutes.

3 Transfer to a bowl. Add the peas, basil, and optional mustard and stir until well combined. Serve immediately.

	CALORIES	PROTEIN	FAT	CARBOHYDRATE	DIETARY FIBER	CALCIUM	SODIUM
per serving	93	7g	0g	19g	8g	63mg	93mg

Roasted Cauliflower and Peas

quick steamed kale
AND MUSHROOMS

 ther hearty greens, such as collards or Swiss chard, work well in this recipe and are just as delicious as kale, so feel free to change it up.

6 cups chopped lacinato or red Russian kale leaves, lightly packed

2 cups sliced mushrooms

1 small onion, chopped

1 tablespoon chopped garlic

1 cup chopped tomatoes

¼ cup chopped fresh basil, lightly packed

1 Dry sauté the kale, mushrooms, onion, and garlic in a large pot over medium-high heat, stirring constantly, for 3–4 minutes.

2 Add the tomatoes, cover, and cook for 1 minute.

3 Add the basil and stir until evenly distributed. Serve hot.

	CALORIES	PROTEIN	FAT	CARBOHYDRATE	DIETARY FIBER	CALCIUM	SODIUM
per serving	80	5g	0g	16g	3g	168mg	50mg

Comfort FOODS

7

Just about all of us have a special go-to dish that reminds us of home, growing up in our mother's or grandmother's kitchen. It's the one dish we can never say no to, regardless of how unhealthy it might be, because when we eat it we feel loved and cared for.

The recipes in this section aren't intended to replace those comfort foods. (Although my dishes are good, they're not good enough to erase your amazing food memories.) But fear not! What my recipes will do is give you a few new options that will seem like a culinary hug. They have a rich and decadent feel to them. Even if you find just one that you adore, you can turn to it the next time you're craving a bit of comfort instead of reaching for something unhealthy.

savory **LENTIL CRÊPES**

rêpes are usually a very indulgent dish and a no-no on a health-conscious diet. But now you can indulge without any guilt. Serve these crêpes with the suggested sauce or stuff them with other recipes from this book, such as Roasted-Garlic Mashed Potatoes (page 69), Braised Red Cabbage with Dried Cherries (page 93), or Quick Steamed Kale and Mushrooms (page 106).

CHEF'S TIP:
Be sure to use split lentils for this recipe. Whole lentils won't work because their outer hull prevents them from absorbing water when they're soaked.

1 cup yellow or red split lentils, soaked in water for 1 hour

2 cups no-salt-added vegetable broth

1 tablespoon chopped fresh basil, chives, tarragon, or thyme

1 tablespoon chopped shallot

1 teaspoon granulated garlic

1 teaspoon granulated onion

1 cup Mint-Cilantro Sauce (page 127)

1 Drain the lentils and put them in a blender. Add the broth, basil, shallot, granulated garlic, and granulated onion and process on high speed until smooth.

2 Preheat a nonstick sauté pan over medium heat.

3 Pour ¼ cup of the lentil batter into the hot pan and spread it into a six-inch round.

4 When the edges begin to brown, use a silicone spatula to flip the crêpe over. Cook for 15 seconds longer, then remove the crêpe from the pan.

5 Repeat the process with the remaining batter.

6 Serve each crêpe with a dollop of the sauce.

	CALORIES	PROTEIN	FAT	CARBOHYDRATE	DIETARY FIBER	CALCIUM	SODIUM
per serving	144	9g	1g	25g	6g	76mg	12mg

Savory Lentil Crêpes

Sweet Lentil Crêpes

sweet **LENTIL CRÊPES**

 he cooked crêpes will have a browned side and a lighter side. Use that to create an eye-catching color contrast when you serve them.

1 cup yellow or red split lentils, soaked in water for 1 hour

2 cups water

1 pitted date

2 teaspoons vanilla extract

¼ teaspoon ground nutmeg or cinnamon

1 cup Berry Marmalade (page 124)

1. Drain the lentils and put them in a blender. Add the water, date, vanilla extract, and nutmeg and process on high speed until smooth.

2. Preheat a nonstick sauté pan over medium heat.

3. Pour ¼ cup of the lentil batter into the hot pan and spread it into a six-inch round.

4. When the edges begin to brown, use a silicone spatula to flip the crêpe over. Cook for 15 seconds longer, then remove the crêpe from the pan.

5. Repeat the process with the remaining batter.

6. Serve each crêpe with a dollop of the marmalade.

	CALORIES	PROTEIN	FAT	CARBOHYDRATE	DIETARY FIBER	CALCIUM	SODIUM
per serving	169	9g	1g	30g	6g	24mg	3mg

lettuce WRAPS

 his dish makes a lovely informal appetizer when it's served family-style. For fancier hors d'oeuvres, use endive leaves instead of lettuce.

2 cups coarsely chopped zucchini

2 cups coarsely chopped carrots

¼ cup raw cashews, toasted (see page 16)

20 whole fresh mint leaves

Juice of 1 lemon

Romaine or butter lettuce leaves, as needed

1 Put the zucchini, carrots, cashews, mint, and lemon juice in a food processor. Process just until finely chopped. Don't allow the mixture to become a paste.

2 Spoon some of the mixture inside each lettuce leaf. Serve immediately.

	CALORIES	PROTEIN	FAT	CARBOHYDRATE	DIETARY FIBER	CALCIUM	SODIUM
per serving	96	3g	4g	14g	3g	45mg	54mg

NORITOS

 his recipe is a cross between burritos and sushi. It's a terrific way to turn leftover grains and veggies into an entirely new dish.

8 nori sheets

4 cups cooked brown rice, quinoa, or buckwheat (see page 19)

2 cups steamed or leftover cooked veggies

1 tablespoon sesame seeds, toasted (see page 16)

2 tablespoons rice vinegar

1 cup Mango-Ginger Dressing (page 51)

1 Put one sheet of nori on a cutting board.

2 Arrange some of the rice, veggies, and sesame seeds on one end of the sheet and sprinkle with some of the vinegar. Roll up the nori sheet.

3 Repeat with the remaining nori sheets, rice, veggies, sesame seeds, and vinegar.

4 Arrange the rolls in a serving dish. Serve with the dressing on the side.

	CALORIES	PROTEIN	FAT	CARBOHYDRATE	DIETARY FIBER	CALCIUM	SODIUM
per serving	278	8g	3g	53g	7g	60mg	13mg

tempeh **TACOS**

 lthough tempeh has a meaty texture, its flavor is an acquired taste for some people. Browning helps make it more palatable.

2 cups crumbled or diced tempeh

1 cup sliced onion

2 cups Bravo Express Salsa (page 129)

8 (six-inch) corn tortillas

1 ripe avocado

Chopped fresh cilantro, for garnish

1 Dry sauté the tempeh and onion in a medium sauté pan over medium heat for 3 minutes.

2 Add the salsa and cook for 2 minutes.

3 Preheat a sauté pan over medium heat. Warm the tortillas one at a time in the hot pan, 30–40 seconds per side.

4 Spoon the tempeh mixture over the warm tortillas. Top with the avocado and garnish with cilantro.

	CALORIES	PROTEIN	FAT	CARBOHYDRATE	DIETARY FIBER	CALCIUM	SODIUM
per serving	721	45g	20g	98g	30g	291mg	45mg

Tempeh Tacos

Tacodillas

TACODILLAS

Put tacos and quesadillas together and you get tacodillas! Other fillings can be used instead of the potatoes, such as Cajun-Roasted Navy Beans and Mushrooms (page 78) or Yellow Curry Lentils (page 77).

12 (six-inch) corn tortillas

½ **recipe** Roasted-Garlic Mashed Potatoes (page 69)

½ **recipe** Chipotle-Almond Salsa (page 126)

1 Preheat the oven to 400 degrees F. Line a baking sheet with parchment paper or a silicone baking mat.

2 Microwave the tortillas until pliable, about 30 seconds. Alternatively, steam the tortillas for 1–2 minutes.

3 Stuff each tortilla with some of the potatoes, then fold in half. Arrange on the lined baking sheet.

4 Bake for 6-7 minutes per side, or until crispy. Serve with the salsa on the side.

	CALORIES	PROTEIN	FAT	CARBOHYDRATE	DIETARY FIBER	CALCIUM	SODIUM
per serving	352	11g	7g	63g	7g	175mg	352mg

YAM empanadas

T he word empanada *roughly translates to "within bread." Basically, the idea is to encase a sweet or savory filling in bread and then bake or deep-fry it. This healthy and delicious version is for a sweet empanada, but the concept might inspire you to create a savory one as well.*

4 large baked yams (see page 18), **peeled**

2 tablespoons unsweetened shredded dried coconut, **toasted** (see page 16)

12 Sweet Lentil Crêpes (page 111)

1 Preheat the oven to 350 degrees F. Line a baking sheet with parchment paper or a silicone baking mat.

2 Put the yams and coconut in a food processor and process for 1 minute.

3 Divide the yam mixture equally among the crêpes, then fold the crêpes over tightly into a half-moon shape.

4 Arrange on the lined baking sheet and bake for 15 minutes.

5 Flip the empanadas over and bake for 10 minutes longer, or until crunchy. Serve immediately.

	CALORIES	PROTEIN	FAT	CARBOHYDRATE	DIETARY FIBER	CALCIUM	SODIUM
per serving	**223**	**6**g	**5**g	**40**g	**3**g	**18**mg	**21**mg

spiced PINE NUTS

Because pine nuts are softer than most other nuts, they will absorb the lime juice better. However, they can be rather pricey. If pine nuts are beyond your budget, sunflower seeds or pumpkin seeds are a less-expensive alternative.

2 cups pine nuts

2 tablespoons lime juice

Chili powder

1 Dry sauté the pine nuts in a large sauté pan over medium heat, stirring constantly.

2 When the nuts begin to brown, add the lime juice and season with chili powder to taste, continuing to stir constantly.

3 Cook for 1 minute longer, then immediately pour the pine nuts into a bowl. Let cool before serving.

	CALORIES	PROTEIN	FAT	CARBOHYDRATE	DIETARY FIBER	CALCIUM	SODIUM
per serving	458	9g	47g	9g	3g	11mg	1mg

Sauces, Salsas, Relishes, AND CHUTNEYS 8

Sauces, when done properly, will always result in juicy, flavorful dishes. A fabulous sauce can elevate a dish from average to outstanding, but a poorly done sauce will do the opposite. Although it's not easy to infuse great flavor into a sauce that's quick and easy to make, I've accomplished the near-impossible and removed the guesswork for you.

All the sauces in this section, with the exception of Bravo Express Salsa (page 129), can be made in large quantities and frozen for up to three months. In addition to the serving suggestions in the individual recipes, you can enjoy these sauces on top of any steamed veggies, whole grains, or potatoes. Cashew Cream (page 122) and Bravo Express Pesto (page 121) are especially good over pasta.

Bravo **EXPRESS PESTO**

 or the best results, use the greenest basil available; avoid any with brown on the leaves. Although the yield for this recipe may seem small, a little goes a long way.

2 cups fresh basil leaves, firmly packed

½ cup fresh spinach leaves, firmly packed

¼ cup no-salt-added vegetable broth

3 tablespoons pine nuts, toasted (see page 16)

3 garlic cloves

1 Put a bowl of ice water next to the stove.

2 Fill a medium pot halfway with water and bring to a boil over high heat. Put the basil in the boiling water for 3 seconds.

3 Using a strainer, immediately remove the basil from the boiling water and dunk it into the ice water for 1 minute. Squeeze the basil dry with paper towels.

4 Put the basil, spinach, broth, pine nuts, and garlic in a blender and process on high speed until smooth. Serve chilled or at room temperature.

	CALORIES	PROTEIN	FAT	CARBOHYDRATE	DIETARY FIBER	CALCIUM	SODIUM
per serving	49	1g	5g	2g	12g	14mg	4mg

CASHEW cream

 his incredibly versatile recipe is reminiscent of creamy Alfredo sauce, so of course it's fabulous on fettuccine.

1 large yellow onion, diced small

2 tablespoons brown rice flour

1 quart no-salt-added vegetable broth

1 cup raw cashews

10 garlic cloves, roasted (see page 15)

1 Dry sauté the onion in a small pot over medium heat, stirring constantly, until browned, 4–5 minutes.

2 Add the flour and cook, stirring constantly, for 30 seconds.

3 Add the broth, cashews, and garlic and bring to a simmer. Cook for 10 minutes.

4 Transfer to a blender and process on high speed until smooth. Serve warm, chilled, or at room temperature.

LEMON-PEPPER CREAM SAUCE: Add the juice of 2 lemons when adding the rice flour to the pot. Season the finished sauce with freshly ground black pepper to taste.

NUTMEG CREAM SAUCE: Stir in 1 teaspoon of freshly grated nutmeg after blending.

SAFFRON CREAM SAUCE: Add a pinch of saffron threads along with the onion.

	CALORIES	PROTEIN	FAT	CARBOHYDRATE	DIETARY FIBER	CALCIUM	SODIUM
per serving	264	1g	5g	18g	2g	34mg	64mg

Cashew Cream

berry MARMALADE

 For this recipe to work properly, the berries must be ripe and sweet.

1 cup fresh strawberries, hulled

1 cup fresh or frozen blackberries

1 cup fresh or frozen blueberries

2 tablespoons unsweetened fruit juice or water

1 cup fresh or frozen raspberries

1. Put the strawberries, blackberries, blueberries, and juice in a medium pot over medium-high heat and cook, stirring constantly, for 4–5 minutes.

2. Add the raspberries and cook for 1 minute longer.

3. Using a slotted spoon, fish out the berries, put them into a medium bowl, and set aside.

4. Cook the remaining juice in the pot over medium-low heat, stirring occasionally, until thick and syrupy, about 10 minutes. As more of the berry liquid evaporates, gradually decrease the heat. The thicker the syrup, the better.

5. Remove the syrup from the heat. Add the reserved berries and stir to combine.

6. Let cool slightly before serving. May also be served chilled or at room temperature.

	CALORIES	PROTEIN	FAT	CARBOHYDRATE	DIETARY FIBER	CALCIUM	SODIUM
per serving	46	1g	1g	9g	2g	11mg	0mg

PECAN gremolata

 his is a fabulous topping for simple starches, such as potatoes, rice, or winter squash.

2 cups coarsely chopped fresh parsley, firmly packed

20 garlic cloves, roasted (see page 15)

20 pecans, toasted (see page 16)

Zest and juice of 2 lemons

1 Put all the ingredients in a food processor and pulse for 15–20 seconds. The mixture should be finely chopped but not blended into a paste.

2 Serve chilled or at room temperature.

	CALORIES	PROTEIN	FAT	CARBOHYDRATE	DIETARY FIBER	CALCIUM	SODIUM
per serving	98	3g	6g	12g	3g	83mg	21mg

chipotle-almond SALSA

 heck the ingredient panel of different brands of chipotle chiles, as some have less sodium than others.

2 cups orange juice

8 ounces canned chipotle chiles

½ cup no-salt-added vegetable broth

½ cup almonds, toasted (see page 16)

1 Put all the ingredients in a blender and process until the desired consistency is achieved.

2 Serve chilled or at room temperature.

	CALORIES	PROTEIN	FAT	CARBOHYDRATE	DIETARY FIBER	CALCIUM	SODIUM
per serving	86	3g	5g	10g	2g	27mg	334mg

mint-cilantro SAUCE

his sauce was inspired by traditional Indian mint-cilantro chutney, which is usually served with naan, a type of Indian bread. Pair this version with Savory Lentil Crêpes (page 108) instead.

1 cup fresh cilantro sprigs, lightly packed

1 cup whole fresh mint leaves, lightly packed

2 tablespoons raw cashews

1 pitted date

Pinch crushed red pepper flakes

1 Put all the ingredients in a blender and process until the desired consistency is achieved.

2 Serve chilled or at room temperature.

	CALORIES	PROTEIN	FAT	CARBOHYDRATE	DIETARY FIBER	CALCIUM	SODIUM
per serving	46	1g	0g	10g	2g	37mg	6mg

raw
CRANBERRY-ORANGE RELISH

Surprise everyone at Thanksgiving with this awesome recipe that's the perfect blend of sweet, tart, and spicy. Just don't tell them it's healthy until after they've licked their plates clean.

4 cups fresh cranberries

Zest and juice of 2 oranges

10 pitted dates

2 tablespoons ground flaxseeds

½ serrano chile **with seeds** (optional)

1 Put all the ingredients in a food processor and process until finely chopped, 15–20 seconds.

2 Serve chilled or at room temperature.

	CALORIES	PROTEIN	FAT	CARBOHYDRATE	DIETARY FIBER	CALCIUM	SODIUM
per serving	117	2g	1g	25g	4g	2mg	1mg

Bravo EXPRESS SALSA

Y *ou can create endless variations of this quick and simple salsa depending on the type of dried chiles you use. Beware that some are hotter than others. If heat isn't your thing, you can omit the chiles, but if your motto is "the hotter the better," feel free to use more than two.*

8 Roma tomatoes, cut in half

½ white onion, sliced thick

4 garlic cloves

2 dried chiles

½ cup chopped fresh cilantro, lightly packed

1 Preheat the oven to 350 degrees F. Line a baking sheet with parchment paper or a silicone baking mat.

2 Arrange the tomatoes, onion, and garlic in a single layer on the lined baking sheet. Bake for 15 minutes.

3 Transfer to a blender. Add the chiles and process for 15–20 seconds.

4 Add the cilantro and pulse just until it's distributed. The salsa should have green specks of cilantro throughout. Serve chilled or at room temperature.

	CALORIES	PROTEIN	FAT	CARBOHYDRATE	DIETARY FIBER	CALCIUM	SODIUM
per serving	23	1g	0g	5g	1g	6mg	7mg

Bravo Express
MARINARA SAUCE

 The combination of the fresh tomatoes and packaged tomatoes gives this sauce the perfect balance of flavor and thickness.

1 yellow onion, diced

4 garlic cloves, chopped

1 tablespoon dried oregano

¼ teaspoon crushed red pepper flakes (optional)

1½ pounds Roma tomatoes, blended and strained

3 cups canned or packaged chopped tomatoes

½ cup fresh basil leaves, lightly packed, chopped

1 Dry sauté the onion, garlic, oregano, and optional red pepper flakes in a large pot over medium-high heat, stirring frequently, until the onion begins to brown.

2 Add the blended tomatoes and chopped tomatoes and bring to a simmer. Cook, stirring occasionally, for 10 minutes.

3 Add the basil and stir until evenly distributed. Serve hot.

	CALORIES	PROTEIN	FAT	CARBOHYDRATE	DIETARY FIBER	CALCIUM	SODIUM
per serving	40	2g	0g	9g	3g	40mg	55mg

sweet onion
AND PINEAPPLE CHUTNEY

 ombining onion and pineapple has been done for centuries. Adopting a healthy diet doesn't mean you have to reinvent the wheel.

1 cup diced onion

1 cup diced pineapple

1 tablespoon brown rice flour

1 cup unsweetened pineapple juice

½ cup no-salt-added vegetable broth

1 Dry sauté the onion and pineapple in a small pot over medium heat, stirring frequently, for 5 minutes.

2 Add the flour and cook, stirring constantly, for 30 seconds.

3 Add the juice and broth and bring to a simmer. Cook, stirring constantly, for 5 minutes. Serve warm, chilled, or at room temperature.

	CALORIES	PROTEIN	FAT	CARBOHYDRATE	DIETARY FIBER	CALCIUM	SODIUM
per serving	75	1g	0g	19g	2g	25mg	8mg

honeydew
CRÈME ANGLAISE

*M*ake sure the honeydew melon is fully ripe when making this recipe, as it's the source of sweetness for this wonderful sauce. Although the sauce is delicious over sliced bananas, berries, and other fresh fruit, it really shines as a topping for baked yams (see page 18).

1 cup full-fat coconut milk

½ vanilla bean, cut in half lengthwise, or 2 teaspoons vanilla extract

1 cup diced ripe honeydew melon

1 kaffir lime leaf, or zest of 1 lime

1 Put the coconut milk and vanilla bean in a small pot and cook over medium-low heat, stirring occasionally, for 5 minutes. Remove from the heat.

2 Scrape the seeds from the vanilla bean into the coconut milk and discard the pod. Let the coconut milk cool to room temperature.

3 Pour the cooled coconut milk into a blender. Add the honeydew melon and kaffir lime leaf and process on high speed for 1 minute. Serve immediately or chilled.

> **CHEF'S TIP:** If you're using vanilla extract, simply put all the ingredients in a blender without heating the coconut milk beforehand.

	CALORIES	PROTEIN	FAT	CARBOHYDRATE	DIETARY FIBER	CALCIUM	SODIUM
per serving	34	0g	2g	3g	0g	4mg	4mg

Snacks & TREATS

9

Having a treat is essential for everyone. Cravings and sweet tooths must be satisfied! Most people think this isn't possible without refined sugar, but that's not true.

In this section you'll find many treats that are sure to surprise you. Keep in mind that they aren't sugar-free, but they are free of refined sugar. What's the difference? With treats that are naturally sweet and don't contain any refined sugar, the flavors are intensified and accentuated, especially when compared to conventional sweets that are merely sugary and lack flavor.

Coconut Bites

coconut **BITES**

 olling these melt-in-your-mouth wonders in toasted coconut isn't absolutely necessary, but it creates a nice visual effect. Bet you can't eat just one!

2 cups diced mango

2 ripe bananas, diced

1 cup unsweetened pineapple juice

½ vanilla bean, cut in half lengthwise, or 1 teaspoon vanilla extract

4 cups unsweetened shredded dried coconut

¾ cup unsweetened shredded dried coconut, toasted (see page 16)

1 Put the mango, bananas, pineapple juice, and vanilla bean in a small pot and cook over medium-low heat for 6 minutes.

2 Scrape the seeds from the vanilla bean into the pot and discard the pod.

3 Transfer the mango mixture to a food processor. Add the 4 cups of coconut and process until smooth and firm.

4 Put the toasted coconut in a small bowl or on a plate.

5 Using a small ice-cream scoop or a spoon, scoop out a small amount of the fruit-and-coconut mixture. Roll it into a 1-inch ball with your hands and then roll it in the toasted coconut. Repeat the process with the remaining mixture.

6 Serve chilled or at room temperature.

	CALORIES	PROTEIN	FAT	CARBOHYDRATE	DIETARY FIBER	CALCIUM	SODIUM
per serving	149	2g	9g	18g	4g	8mg	6mg

vanilla POACHED PEARS

 Although vanilla beans can be expensive, their tiny black seeds give this dish a stunning appearance.

2 quarts unsweetened pineapple juice

4 ripe pears, peeled

Zest and juice of 2 oranges

1 vanilla bean, cut in half lengthwise, or 1 tablespoon vanilla extract

1 Put the pineapple juice, pears, orange zest and juice, and vanilla bean in a medium pot.

2 Cut a circular piece of parchment paper that matches the diameter of the pot. Put the parchment circle on top of the pears (this will keep them in contact with the liquid so they cook evenly) and bring to a boil over medium-high heat.

3 Decrease the heat to medium-low, keeping the liquid at a gentle simmer, and cook until you can insert a paring knife in and out of the pears without any resistance. Remove the pears from the liquid and set them aside.

4 Scrape the seeds from the vanilla bean into the pot and discard the pod.

5 Put 1 cup of the liquid into a small sauté pan and cook over medium heat until it thickens into a syrup, about 5 minutes. Drizzle the syrup over the pears. Serve immediately.

	CALORIES	PROTEIN	FAT	CARBOHYDRATE	DIETARY FIBER	CALCIUM	SODIUM
per serving	360	3g	0g	93g	11g	98mg	33mg

spicy apple **CIDER**

 ost traditional ciders tend to be overly sweet. For this recipe, a trio of sweet, sour, and spicy ingredients creates an explosion of flavor.

1 gallon unsweetened apple juice

Zest and juice of 2 oranges

Zest and juice of 2 lemons

2 Granny Smith apples, diced

2 tablespoons mulling spices

2 serrano chiles, cut in half lengthwise (don't remove the seeds)

1　Put all the ingredients in a large pot and bring to a boil over medium-high heat. Decrease the heat to low and simmer for 20 minutes.

2　Strain before serving. Serve hot, warm, or chilled.

	CALORIES	PROTEIN	FAT	CARBOHYDRATE	DIETARY FIBER	CALCIUM	SODIUM
per serving	217	1g	1g	54g	3g	9mg	13mg

BLUEBERRY-LIME *truffles*

Who doesn't love truffles!

1½ cups old-fashioned rolled oats

1 cup blueberries

10 pitted dates

Zest and juice of 1 lime

2 cups raw cashews, toasted (see page 16) and chopped

1 Put the oats in a food processor and pulse for 15 seconds. Transfer to a small bowl and set aside.

2 Put the blueberries, dates, and lime zest and juice in the food processor and process for 10 seconds.

3 Add the oats all at once and process until well incorporated, about 15 seconds.

4 Transfer to a medium bowl and let rest for 30 minutes.

5 Divide the mixture into twenty pieces and roll each piece into a one-inch ball.

6 Put the cashews on a plate or in a small bowl and roll each ball in them until evenly coated. Serve immediately or chilled.

	CALORIES	PROTEIN	FAT	CARBOHYDRATE	DIETARY FIBER	CALCIUM	SODIUM
per serving	543	15g	28g	64g	8g	56mg	12mg

Blueberry-Lime Truffles

coconut RICE PUDDING

Forbidden black rice got its name because it was once reserved only for Chinese emperors, thus making it forbidden for everyone else. You can substitute another rice in this recipe, but you'll be missing the luscious deep-purple color of the forbidden rice. The multiple layers of coconut flavor make this dessert very rich, creamy, and tasty.

1½ cups forbidden black rice

6 cups unsweetened apple juice

1 teaspoon peeled and chopped fresh ginger

1 young coconut, or 1 (8-ounce) can or bottle coconut water with pulp

1 cup full-fat coconut milk

¾ cup unsweetened shredded dried coconut, toasted (see page 16)

1. Put the rice, apple juice, and ginger in a medium pot and bring to a boil over medium-high heat. Decrease the heat to low, cover, and cook for 1 hour.

2. While the rice is cooking, open the young coconut using a sharp knife with a heavy blade and pour the coconut water into a large bowl.

3. Scoop out the coconut pulp with a spoon. Cut it into strips and add it to the coconut water.

4. Add the cooked rice, coconut milk, and dried coconut and stir until well combined.

5. Let cool for 1 hour at room temperature, then chill in the refrigerator for at least 8 hours before serving.

CHEF'S TIP:
When all the ingredients are first combined, the mixture will seem too soupy. Don't worry! The pudding will thicken to the right consistency after it's been thoroughly chilled for at least 8 hours.

	CALORIES	PROTEIN	FAT	CARBOHYDRATE	DIETARY FIBER	CALCIUM	SODIUM
per serving	356	3g	11g	63g	4g	26mg	19mg

baked SPICED APPLES

T art apples work better than sweet apples for this recipe because their flavor is more balanced when they're baked. These apples are delicious served hot for breakfast with oatmeal stuffed in the center. They're also wonderful cold, served on their own or with celery sticks on the side.

8 Granny Smith, Gala, or Fuji apples

½ teaspoon ground cinnamon

½ teaspoon ground nutmeg

1 Preheat the oven to 350 degrees F.

2 Core the apples using an apple corer. Rub some of the cinnamon and nutmeg in the center of each apple.

3 Put the apples in a baking dish and bake for 25–30 minutes, until tender. Let cool slightly before serving.

	CALORIES	PROTEIN	FAT	CARBOHYDRATE	DIETARY FIBER	CALCIUM	SODIUM
per serving	162	0g	0g	44g	10g	43mg	0mg

date-apricot **PASTE**

 se this sweet spread the same way you would use apple butter. It pairs well with sliced apples or pineapple wedges and is great smeared on rice cakes.

2 cups unsweetened pineapple juice

½ cup pitted dates

½ cup dried apricots

2 teaspoons vanilla extract

1 Put the pineapple juice, dates, apricots, and vanilla extract in a medium pot and bring to a simmer over medium heat. Decrease the heat to low and cook for 10 minutes.

2 Transfer to a food processor or blender and process until smooth. Serve warm, chilled, or at room temperature.

	CALORIES	PROTEIN	FAT	CARBOHYDRATE	DIETARY FIBER	CALCIUM	SODIUM	
per serving	174	2g	0g	43g	3g	34mg	5mg	

mango-coconut ICE CREAM

 Using very ripe mangoes is the key to this wonderful treat.

4 cups frozen mango chunks

1 frozen banana, broken into large pieces

½ cup full-fat coconut milk

½ cup unsweetened shredded dried coconut, toasted (see page 16)

1 Let the mango and banana rest at room temperature for 5 minutes to thaw slightly.

2 Put the mango, banana, and coconut milk in a high-speed blender with a tamper or in a food processor and process until the consistency of soft-serve ice cream.

3 Add the coconut and process or pulse for a few seconds, just until evenly distributed. Serve immediately.

> **CHEF'S TIP:** You can put this ice cream in the freezer for up to 15 minutes to hold it before serving, but if it's in the freezer any longer than this, it will start to get too hard and become too difficult to scoop or eat.

	CALORIES	PROTEIN	FAT	CARBOHYDRATE	DIETARY FIBER	CALCIUM	SODIUM
per serving	**331**	**1**g	**16**g	**45**g	**4**g	**1**mg	**72**mg

Peach-Blueberry Sorbet

peach-blueberry **SORBET**

I f you purchase frozen fruit from the supermarket, this recipe will be super-easy to prepare. But if you prefer to use fresh fruit, buy it at the peak of the season, then cut it and freeze it before using.

4 cups frozen sliced peaches

2 cups frozen blueberries

¼ cup bottled unsweetened peach juice

¼ cup chopped fresh mint, lightly packed

1 Put all the ingredients in a high-speed blender with a tamper or in a food processor and process until smooth.

2 Serve immediately.

CHEF'S TIP: You can put this sorbet in the freezer for up to 15 minutes to hold it before serving, but if it's in the freezer any longer than this, it will start to get too hard and become too difficult to scoop or eat.

	CALORIES	PROTEIN	FAT	CARBOHYDRATE	DIETARY FIBER	CALCIUM	SODIUM
per serving	**145**	**2**g	**1**g	**37**g	**5**g	**40**mg	**12**mg

banana-walnut
ICE CREAM

 t's best to eat all of this splendid dessert as soon as it's made, as putting it in the freezer will turn it rock hard.

4 frozen bananas, broken into large pieces

¼ cup unsweetened almond milk

½ teaspoon ground cinnamon

½ cup walnuts, toasted (see page 16) and coarsely chopped

1 Put the bananas in a high-speed blender with a tamper or in a food processor.

2 Add the almond milk and cinnamon and process until the consistency of soft-serve ice cream.

3 Transfer to a bowl, add the walnuts, and stir with a silicone spatula until evenly distributed. Serve immediately.

	CALORIES	PROTEIN	FAT	CARBOHYDRATE	DIETARY FIBER	CALCIUM	SODIUM
per serving	413	7g	21g	59g	9g	103mg	26mg

melon skewers
WITH ORANGE SYRUP

 f you like, try other fruits in addition to or instead of the melons, although I think nutmeg pairs especially well with melons.

Zest and juice of 2 oranges

¼ teaspoon ground nutmeg

1 ripe honeydew melon, cut into 1-inch cubes

1 ripe cantaloupe, cut into 1-inch cubes

1 Put the orange zest and juice and nutmeg in a small pot and cook over low heat until the liquid is syrupy and reduced to one-quarter of the original volume, 4–5 minutes.

2 Push bamboo skewers through the melon cubes and arrange the skewers on a plate.

3 Drizzle the orange syrup over the skewers. Serve immediately.

	CALORIES	PROTEIN	FAT	CARBOHYDRATE	DIETARY FIBER	CALCIUM	SODIUM
per serving	172	3g	1g	43g	5g	31mg	68mg

INDEX

BookPuBlishing Co.

books that educate, inspire, and empower

To find your favorite books on plant-based cooking and nutrition,
raw-foods cuisine, and healthy living, visit:

BookPubCo.com

Bravo!

Ramses Bravo

978-1-57067-269-9 • $19.95

The Pleasure Trap

Alan Goldhamer, DC
Douglas J. Lisle, PhD

978-1-57067-197-5 • $14.95

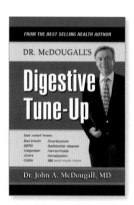

**Dr. McDougall's
Digestive Tune-Up**

John McDougall, MD

978-1-57067-184-5 • $19.95

**The Health Promoting
Cookbook**

Alan Goldhamer, DC

978-1-57067-024-4 • $14.95

Purchase these titles from your favorite book source or buy them directly from:
Book Publishing Company • PO Box 99 • Summertown, TN 38483 • 1-888-260-8458

Free shipping and handling on all orders